Y2K for Women

HOW TO PROTECT YOUR HOME
AND FAMILY IN THE COMING CRISIS

Karen Anderson
Founder, Y2KWomen

THOMAS NELSON PUBLISHERS®
Nashville

Published in Nashville, Tennessee, by Thomas Nelson, Inc.

Published in association with the literary agency of Alive Communications, 1465 Kelly Johnson Blvd., Suite 320, Colorado Springs, CO 80920.

Originally published by Sovereign Press, Inc.

This publication is designed to provide general information in regard to the subject matter covered. It is distributed with the understanding that neither the author nor publisher is engaged in rendering legal, medical, or other professional services. It should not be utilized as a substitute for professional legal, medical, or technical advice or services if a professional is required.

ISBN 0-7394-0467-9

Printed in the United States of America.

This book is dedicated to my husband, Steve, and my daughters, Kelly and Stephanie, and to the memory of my father, Paul S. Gilbride. It is also dedicated to the many women around the world who, just as I am, are working diligently to protect their families and be prepared for any emergency. Proverbs 31.

Contents

Contents

Acknowledgments

There is a verse in Scripture that says, "For everyone to whom much is given, from him much will be required" (Luke 12:48 NKJV). I am one of those people who have been given much and blessed in many ways. I'd like to take this opportunity to publicly thank those people in my life who have been there with me through thick and thin (literally!). My special thanks goes . . .

First, to my Sailing Crew. It is hard to explain what a wonderful experience it is to live with 11 women in only 65 feet of space for a whole week, but the Young Life sailing trip in the San Juan Islands was just that. Our "crew" was exceptional: Evette Gentry, Tina Gilchrist, Tami Peterson, Jill Stallard, Debbie Samples, Joann Tippery, Brenda Huckins, Ina Bartell, Cindy Taylor, Dana Thompson. And our Captain Kim Edy and his wife, Dona, were extraordinary, to say the least. It was an incredible opportunity for us as women to spend time together and grow deeper in our relationships and in our faith. What a blessing. Thank you all for loving me.

To my good friends Debbie Miller and Terri Riehl. Although we are located east, west and in the middle, I appreciate how our friendships have grown over the years. Thank you, my friends.

To my "best friend since sixth grade" Ellen Avery. Thanks for always being there when I've been out on a limb. (I think I have never gotten over the ropes course at YL's Champion!)

To Sharon North. Thanks for hanging in there with me during the really difficult times. You embody loveliness and inspire me to remember that even during Y2K there will still be beauty.

To my church family, my special thanks. In particular my care group: The Delphs, Gilchrists, Hudsons, Ortizes, Jensens, Gentrys, Stallards, Samples and Wileys.

To Marlain and Mary Liggett. How would I ever get through a deadline without you being there? Thank you for being such servants to me.

To Dale Smith, a.k.a. the Bishop of Colleyville. How I appreciate you! Your passion in life is always an example to me. Thank you for having a pastor's heart.

My thanks to the many wonderful people I have met as I have learned about Y2K. Each has contributed in their own way, and all with the goal of helping others. Ed Yourdon, Mike Hyatt (editing your book spurred me on to create something to help women—I am grateful for your research), James and LeeDee Stevens, Patrick D'Acre, and Shaunti Feldhahn (thanks for taking the time to do my foreword!).

To my buddies on the "Dream Team": Craig Smith, Tony Keyes, Ed Meagher, Tim Wilson as well as those behind the scenes people who have been a tremendous support: David Bradshaw, Darci North and Paloma O'Riley.

To everyone who has had a hand in production: Ginny Youmans, Mark Donaldson, Stanley, Jeff Jensen and staff at SAS, John Finn, Dan Poynter, Sandy Hidler, Danny Turner and Christina (you guys made me look great!), Leslie Mitchamore. And a very special thanks to Christine Silk, Karen Hayes, Wendy Huckeba, for their writing help—I couldn't have done it without you all!

To Greg Johnson, my literary agent at Alive Communications, for his help and patience in working out the details of getting this book to the best publisher in lightning speed. And to Thomas Nelson Publishers for their extraordinary efforts in fast tracking this book to get it out to the public in record breaking time.

To David Dunham. Thanks for having confidence in me! Your support has always been invaluable.

To Bruce Tippery. Who would have ever thought I'd end up advising women on survival and preparedness? Thanks for still being there.

To Steve and Jill Stallard. Lord knows I couldn't survive without Stallard and Co. CPA's (Cindy, Eva and Sally) who have walked with me through fire (the IRS!) and have been so supportive.

To my very special friends who have supported me over the years: Jay Abraham, Mac and Marji Ross, Susan Berkley, Rick Popowitz, David Deutsch, Bob Serling, Janet Switzer, Michelle Quinn, Joel Roberts, Mitch Axelrod, Farida Karimi, Bill Cantrell (I guess I finally found my direction!).

To Gary North. Thank you for our friendship.

To Audri (and Jim) Lanford, my thanks for being there through the tough times and for believing in me even when I didn't always believe in myself. Without your "tech support" this never would have happened!

To Sissi Haner. The linchpin in all that I have done has rested on Sissi, my awesome Webmistress and good friend. I can never repay her for her dedication but I know tens of thousands of people have been helped by her hard work and efforts. Youdabest, kid!

To my two dear friends in our unlikely trio—Evette and Tina. How could I ask for better (not to mention unusual!) friends?

Finally, I wish to thank my family: my brother, Scott Gilbride, and his wife, Anne, and Lindsay, Mary Lacey, and Annabelle. And my sister-in-law, Peggy Borsay, mother-in-law, Carol Anderson, and my mom, Ky Gilbride—all women who have faced adversity with style and grace.

Kelly and Stephanie have given up so much of themselves to let me do this work. Many sacrifices have been made to get this book written. I can't thank them enough for all of their love.

And last but not least, I want to thank my husband, Steve. I could not ask for a more supportive husband and even though he said "for better or worse" I know he got more than he bargained for! God knew exactly what I needed when he gave me you. From the bottom of my heart, thank you for everything.

Foreword

Most of the Y2K books published today seem to concentrate on the technical issues surrounding the Year 2000 problem, discussing embedded chip telemetry and COBOL code at length and giving short shrift to the real life, bottom line questions we all want to know: *exactly how can I help my family get ready?*

Don't get me wrong, it is extremely important that we understand the very real reasons for Y2K concern, so that we can come to an informed decision on the subject. But after months of seeing other books say things like "power supplies may be disrupted, therefore check into alternative sources of power and light," I want to stand on a chair and yell, "What kind of alternatives?! Help me out here . . . I don't have time to do all this research!" Frankly, at the end of a long day I wouldn't know a diesel 500 watt generator from a detachable solar lamp module.

Thank goodness I don't have to. Over the course of the past three years, Karen Anderson has done all the research for me, and continues where the other books leave off. Frankly, although my own book *Y2K: The Millennium Bug—A Balanced Christian Response* has been well-received, it too deals with more "external" issues such as the evidence behind Y2K and the importance of serving others if we face disruptions. In fact, until I read Karen's book, I had always secretly felt unprepared to deal with many of the rubber-meets-the-road, practical issues. Not anymore. Karen has clearly explained not only the key possibilities for Y2K disruptions, but also the realistic "how-to's" for dealing with them, in the sort of practical and interesting terms that make family Y2K decisions easy.

In the face of all the Y2K hype out there, we need this very down-to-earth and engaging book. We need something written by an informed non-technical person that will explain the essential Y2K issues for other similarly non-technical people. We need something from a wife and mother that just comes out and answers the unasked practical and emotional questions that we women are all thinking about anyway. We need someone who, when people start panicking about cashing out their 401k plans, can say, "It's okay. Take a deep breath—we will get through this!" Most of all, we need someone who assures us that since no one can possibly know what Y2K will bring, our preparatory actions are only prudent . . . the millennial equivalent of fire insurance.

I commend Karen for bringing Y2K down to earth, confronting it with faith and balance, and providing feasible and practical advice that is accessible and relevant to us as women. Today, we have credible evidence that Y2K could actually cause real problems. We can all pray that Y2K is no big deal, but we need to get our families and communities ready, just in case.

—Shaunti Feldhahn

Letter from Karen

In the spring of 1998, after becoming increasingly frustrated with the fact that nobody was writing anything that was reader-friendly to women, I ended up writing something specifically designed to explain the year 2000 problem to women that addressed many women's concerns and issues. Sort of on a lark, I decided to put it on the Internet (since it was basically free!) to see if there was any response.

Well, the response was overwhelming!

Since I launched my Web page in June 1998 (www.y2kwomen.com), I've fielded thousands of heartfelt messages from women, and more than a few men, grandparents and kids seeking information about how to prepare for Y2K. What started as a part-time project mushroomed, seemingly overnight, into something so huge I couldn't possibly give each question a personal and worthwhile response. So I began a free online newsletter, or an e-zine (electronic magazine), called "Dear Karen . . . Advice for Women on the Concerns and Effects of the Year 2000 Problem." It is a Dear Abby-like column where many women have written in their questions. They're excellent questions that deserve an answer.

However, I quickly figured out that while I was trying to communicate Y2K to women who didn't have computer experience or access, I was using the Internet to try and reach those women. Duh!

So, I wrote this book.

In the pages that follow, I have condensed many of the frequently asked questions and worries that were sent to the "Dear Karen . . ." section of my Y2KWomen Website. I've consulted with experts, searching and researching for reliable, reasonable answers, and I offer those answers here, in the hope that they'll help you and your loved ones prepare yourselves—rationally, practically, without panic and with good, solid judgment intact—for what is increasingly being referred to as the "Y2K Crisis." (Now, if you are intimately familiar with my Website, I need to ask your indulgence, as this is new material to many. I review Y2K in the beginning of the book to make sure that everybody is up to speed on what the problem is. I figure, if people don't understand the problem, then they are unlikely to be motivated to do anything about it.)

Is Y2K really a crisis? As you've probably noticed, it depends on whom you ask. But since I have many roles (wife, mother, daughter, daughter-in-law, sister-in-law, church member, community member, neighbor, etc.) I've decided to take what seems to be the most prudent route to protect my loved ones: Prepare for the worst and hope and pray for the best. As the saying goes, "You don't have to worry about the train you see coming. It's the one you don't see that can really hurt you!" Whether you believe Y2K will be a crisis or a fizzle, I'm a firm believer that we would all be wise to have some sort of plan to take care of ourselves—physically, financially, emotionally and socially—just in case the lights go out, the heat (or air conditioner) shuts down, the phone goes dead, the faucet runs dry, the ATM machine forgets who you are, and the grocery store shelves go bare.

Do you think all this sounds impossible? Are you feeling confident "somebody" will get it fixed before the ball drops in Times Square at midnight on December 31, 1999? Don't bank on it.

The bad news is, the chairman of the House subcommittee on government management in Washington, D.C., said in a recent report that federal agencies are way behind in getting the computer bug out of their systems, and at the present rate some may not be up and running optimally until the year 2034! The good news is, preparing yourself and your family for this sort of thing can be easy—and in my view it's something we should have been doing all along anyway, as a kind of insurance policy, for any kind of emergency, whether natural or man-made. The bottom line is this: with God's strength, we will get through this by working together. With the information in this book, I hope you'll feel inspired to get started and the sooner, the better. Finally, remember this: the only way to eat an elephant is one bite at a time!

With warmest wishes,

Karen Anderson

Introduction

It was about three years ago that I was sitting at my kitchen table after dinner talking with a friend who had come into town to visit. The kids had gone to do their homework, and my husband, Steve, our friend Gary, and I were discussing some of the issues Steve was facing in his job as a technology consultant for the insurance industry. Steve started talking about the "Millennium Bug" and how the date change was going to wreak havoc in computers. In fact, he said he believed from his research that about a third of the independent insurance agencies would go out of business because of this problem. Gary had heard of the problem, but I thought it was all kind of strange. How could just changing the date from 1999 to 2000 put people out of business?

While we continued talking that night, I asked, "Won't Bill Gates come in and fix the problem with all his money and resources?" I figured Microsoft would come out with new software, fix the problem, and make a ton *more* money. It seemed simple enough to me. And anyway, I couldn't see how it would impact me. My major inconvenience with a new year is always forgetting to write the new year in the date space when I write checks at the grocery store!

The guys were acting as if this was a big deal and that it was going to get worse, but it didn't sound that way to me. When they started talking about how it could affect me and my household (I have two teenage daughters), I thought they were totally crazy. The things they were talking about happening seemed like stuff out of a bad sci-fi movie—*The Computer That Destroyed the World*.

While we were getting ready for bed that night, expecting Steve to reassure me, I said, "Honey, you don't think any of those things will really happen, do you?" He sighed and said, "Yeah, I think they will."

Since that night, I've spent a lot of time looking into what this problem really is, what it means, and whether or not I should be concerned about it for my family. But one of the things I've found is that Y2K information is not especially "user-friendly" to women. It's mostly written by men to men (or to businesses where they think more "male").

The more I talked with women about this problem, the more I realized that there were a lot of women out there who wanted to understand more about it but didn't want to wade through all the "techie" stuff. There were also lots of women who were getting into serious arguments with their husbands. The men wanted to do all sorts of "crazy" things (like sell their houses and liquidate their life savings) and their wives didn't understand why they were reacting the way they were! So I decided to put together something that was easy to understand and that gave women some options to determine for themselves what, if anything, they should do.

I also realized some of the things that needed to be done to protect their families were things that should be done, *no matter whether people believed the Y2K problem was true or not.*

The other thing I've found is, I believe John Gray was right on target when he wrote his book, *Men Are from Mars and Women Are from Venus!* Women communicate differently and have very different needs and ways of seeing the world than men do. And men, for some strange reason, can't seem to figure out how to communicate with women (it seems so simple to me!). I think this is particularly true when Mars and Venus look at Y2K!

Here's a story I heard that I think illustrates the point.

A man was taking his morning jog along the beach early one day. He came across an old bottle poking out of the sand. It was colorful, and he picked it up and began to rub the sand off of it. Suddenly, out popped a genie. The genie said, "I am so grateful to get out of that bottle that I will grant you one wish."

The man thought for awhile and finally said, "I have

always wanted to go to Hawaii. I've never been able to go because airplanes are much too frightening for me. On a boat, I become very seasick. So I wish for a road to be built from here to Hawaii."

The genie thought for a few minutes and finally said, "No, I don't think I can do that. Just think of all the work involved. Consider all the pilings needed to hold up a highway and how deep they would have to go to reach the bottom of the ocean. Imagine all the pavement needed. No, that is just too much to ask."

The man thought for a few minutes and then told the genie, "There is one other thing I have always wanted. I would like to be able to understand women. What makes them laugh and cry, why are they temperamental, why are they so difficult to get along with? Basically, what makes them tick?"

The genie considered this for a few moments and said, "So, do you want two lanes or four?"

The point of my story is that women and men see the world differently. (Sometimes it might be easier to build a bridge over the ocean!) They evaluate problems differently, and they don't always agree on what the "solution" should be. This is especially true when you look at the Y2K problem. I've talked to a lot of women—married, single, with children and without children— and they want to know what Y2K is all about. The problem is, they're not necessarily getting useful information from the men in their lives, such as their husbands, boyfriends and brothers, or they may find that talking to men about such a big issue is an exasperating and frustrating experience.

You see, many men are just not good at understanding a problem from a woman's point of view. You probably know a man for whom it is impossible to sit down and simply listen to what you have to say, without interrupting, without judging, without offering unwanted advice. Instead, a lot of men have a communication style that's something like a teacher lecturing to a student. Have you ever noticed how men will sometimes pour knowledge into the heads of their listeners (especially when the listeners are women) without bothering to find out how much their listeners know or care about already? Often, when a woman asks a man to understand a problem she's having, the first thing out of his mouth is some solution, along the lines of, "Well, you ought to do such-and-such . . ." Maybe all she wanted was a sympathetic ear, someone to say, "I understand what you're going through," not a lecture on how to do things.

I know there are many women out there who want to know about Y2K and who want to know what they should do. But they are frustrated talking to their husbands or partners who already "know" the answers (or who think they know the answers!). Many women are frustrated with men who want to tell them what to do and how to do it—without listening and appreciating their concerns. A lot of women need the chance to sound out their own concerns about Y2K. They want to come to their own conclusions about it and decide if and how they want to prepare for the coming millennium change. As you can imagine, this is not something that sits well with a man who thinks he's got it all figured out.

I know this is not true of all men—there are some great, sensitive guys out there! But in the rush of living in the day-to-day hectic world, a lot of times communication is one of the things that go out the window.

On the other side, there are many women who, after hearing about Y2K, "get" the big picture from the very beginning. They almost intuitively understand how precarious things are since so much of what goes on in our everyday lives is interrelated and, for the most part, our lives are controlled by behind the scenes computers. But many women are saying their husbands or boyfriends are taking "the Ostrich approach"—sticking their heads in the sand and hoping the problem won't happen, will go away or someone will fix it without their having to do anything.

Over the last three years, I've done a lot of research on the year 2000 problem. I've read as much about it as I could get my hands on. And I've talked to a lot of women—regular women like you and me—who want to know what it's all about. Now mind you, my degrees are in psychology, social work and family therapy, and I am not exactly a computer-head. In fact, I'm lucky if I can navigate my way around my own computer just to get basic things done like writing, checking my email and balancing my checkbook!

However, I believe my lack of computer expertise is an advantage for you because I've waded through all the technical stuff (and pulled out a few handfuls of hair during the process). In fact, I've driven my husband a little crazy in the process! Actually, part of his job is to take technical information and make it understandable to "normal" people (I'm afraid he doesn't always put me in that category!). I've tried to reduce all this information down and put it into its most simple, clear and easy to understand terms so I can understand it and hopefully, that may help you to understand it, too.

This book is designed to help women and the men in their lives to communicate, cooperate and prepare for the future together. If you are married or in a committed relationship, this book is for you. I will show you how to think about Y2K, and how to prepare for it in the context of your personal relationships and family life.

If you are single, you are no less in need of this book. After all, single women need good information about Y2K because, at the very least, they have themselves to take care of. Many single women also have children and elderly parents to look after, and keeping their families safe is no less important for them than it is for married women.

So when reading this book, take into context that I am married and have kids and therefore I write as a mom with concerns for her family, but take out of it what you need for your own particular situation.

"I Don't Want to Think About This!"

Before I tell you what Y2K is all about, I want to spend a few moments to tell you about something else: The curious tendency of humans to rationalize or ignore unpleasant truths. It's natural to tune out things that are unpleasant. It's a survival mechanism. If you worried about every "doom and gloom" prediction that came your way, you'd have no time to do anything else. But I'm going to tell you why Y2K isn't just another crackpot theory, and why credible, professional experts from all walks of life are taking it seriously, and why you should, too.

Imagine that you lived next to a mountain, and some people told you, "You'd better leave this area, because that mountain is going to explode soon." Would you: (a) refuse to move, because you believe nothing bad is going to happen (after all, that mountain has been the same way since your great-granddaddy's time), (b) be tempted to move, but stay put because you're worried about looking like a paranoid fool if nothing happens, or (c) move anyway, just to be on the safe side. Which would you choose?

Well, you'd probably say it depends on things like who the people are who are predicting the explosion, what their evidence is, whether anyone else is taking them seriously, and so forth. Your choice might be very different from that of other people, including your closest friends and relatives, because each individual brings a unique perspective and personal way of calculating risk.

But what if I told you the mountain is Mt. St. Helen's? Would that influence your choice? You're probably thinking: "Of course, it would! I'd definitely choose to leave. Everybody knows Mt. St. Helen's did erupt!" That's true, but before it erupted, nobody knew for sure that it was going to do so. That's why a lot of people chose to stay, and, sadly, they paid for that decision with their lives.

We can sit back and feel smug that we would never be so stupid and complacent. But, after all, hindsight is always 20/20. Before May 18, 1980, a lot of people living at the foot of Mt. St. Helen's didn't believe it was going to erupt, because it hadn't done so in their lifetimes or even as far back as their grandparents' lifetimes. But just because something hasn't happened in the past doesn't mean the future will be the same way. Despite the warnings, those folks who stayed at Mt. St. Helen's didn't have the luxury of a second chance when the ash washed over their homes.

Y2K is different. Because it is a fixed deadline, you have the luxury of planning for difficult times. I want to keep you from making the same mistake, with regard to this impending crisis, that a few people did with Mt. St. Helen's with disastrous consequences. It is so easy to dismiss Y2K as "only a theory," just like some of the unfortunate residents dismissed the scientists' predictions that Mt. St. Helen's was ready to blow. That's why I think it's important that you at least consider the issues concerning the Y2K problem, and then make up your own mind about whether you should take even just a few small steps to keep you and your family safe. As you'll see, I'm not recommending anything terribly radical or expensive or time-consuming. Just little steps you can take, one at a time, at your own pace, until you've built a safety net to carry you and your family through any disaster—natural or man-made—that may come your way.

How Does the Y2K Problem Affect Me?

The Y2K problem sounds like a trivial little problem that shouldn't affect you, doesn't it? Well, it does affect you in ways that aren't always obvious. Think about how many things in your life depend on a computer knowing what date it is. All of your insurance policies, your bank accounts, your pension plans, even your paycheck are heavily computerized and date-sensitive. If the computer has the date wrong, it may accidentally cancel your insurance policy or prevent you from filing a claim. You may not be able to withdraw or deposit money at your bank when you need to. The interest on your pension plans may be calculated incorrectly, costing you lots of money and time to get it fixed. Your paycheck may be late or lost, and you may not get paid what's owed to you. And that's just what might happen in the financial industry.

There are other industries that affect your day-to-day living. Power companies are heavily computerized. If the gas or electricity goes down because of a computer malfunction, how will you heat your house and run your appliances? How will you cook food? Phone companies are heavily computerized. If there's no phone service because the computers controlling the switchboards have crashed when 2000 comes, how will you call for help if you need it?

Transportation systems and retail businesses are heavily computerized. In fact, some experts recommend that people avoid flying right around the time when the millennium changes, just to be sure the automated flight systems don't cause problems when "99" flips over to "00."

You think the government is on top of this? Don't bet on it! The *Wall Street Journal* (3/3/98, p. A18) reported that the Federal Aviation Administration (FAA) is already 15 years behind schedule in upgrading the regular equipment it uses to conduct airplanes in and out of airports. Worse yet, the FAA "lags woefully behind in repairing date-related computer glitches and almost certainly won't have the necessary fixes completed by the millennium"– fixes that are crucial if the government is serious about "preventing the system from collapsing in a heap . . ."

Airplanes are a vital part of our transportation network, but they're just one piece of it. If the trucking, train or shipping industries face the same problems as the airlines (and they are all heavily computerized), we may have serious delays getting food, fuel, clothing and medical supplies.

If you have very small children, think of the inconvenience this could cause. The grocery store may not have the diapers or formula your baby needs. If someone in your family gets sick, you may have a hard time getting a prescription filled because shipments of medications have been delayed or canceled. This could be life-threatening if you or a loved one depends on daily medication to stay alive. You may have difficulties getting the basic necessities for your family if our transportation network goes into temporary shock. All because of a tiny computer glitch.

Maybe you'll be lucky when the date switches over to 2000, and the computers in your immediate area will work perfectly. That still doesn't mean you'll be unaffected. Computers are all interconnected on a worldwide network. If a computer in another state or country gives the computers in your area wrong information, it could cause those computers to malfunction as well. You've heard of a computer virus, right? Well, think of the Y2K problem as a virus that could cause even properly programmed computers to crash or generate wrong information if the computers are not outfitted with the proper detectors. (Why do you think they call it a "bug"!) All this could have disastrous consequences for you and everyone else in this country.

Dr. Edward Yardeni, chief economist at Deutsche Morgan Grenfell, a global investment banking firm, testified to members of a congressional subcommittee in November 1997 that the Y2K problem "is a very serious threat to the U.S. economy." He started out predicting that there would be a 40% risk of a worldwide recession that will last at least twelve months starting January 2000. Then Yardeni upped that figure to a 60% chance. At the time of this writing, he is now saying 70%! "It could be as severe as the 1973-74 global recession," he estimates. "If the supply of information is disrupted, many economic activities will be impaired, if not entirely halted."

This means that ordinary things, like applying for loans or credit, withdrawing money, or just being able to plan a basic household budget for a few months might be chaotic and uncertain. You might see the prices of necessities like food and gas skyrocket as people try to deal with a recession.

Private companies, such as those that provide you with the goods and services you use every day, are at risk, too. I ran across an article last year in *Barron's*, a business weekly published by Dow Jones. It cites a study by Forrester Research which found that "large companies have underestimated by 25% the work required for Y2K assessment, repair and testing."

Think about what this means to you. If, by the year 2000, the big food companies, pharmaceutical companies, banks, credit card issuers, insurance companies and hospitals aren't quite finished fixing their computers, and those computers crash or give wrong information, we could all suffer the consequences. Those consequences might include anything from not being able to buy your regular groceries, to having to wait much longer to get medical care while the hospital attempts to locate your or your children's records and manually deal with everybody who needs medical attention. That could be disastrous in an emergency.

If you think I'm overstating the seriousness of the problem, ask yourself how many times you've tried to do business with a company, only to have them tell you, "Could you call back later? Our computers are down right now, and we can't do anything for you." I can't count how many times this has happened to me, when I've called my doctor, the bank, the credit card company, the utility company, the phone company or tried to order goods over the phone. That tells you how heavily dependent we all are on computers for routine, day-to-day interactions. Imagine if the computers you deal with weren't down for just a few hours, but a few weeks or even months. Imagine how that could cause your everyday activities to slow down to a crawl or even grind to a halt while folks scramble to fix their computers and get them back online. In the meantime, your family is left needing basic things like food, medicine, clothes, fuel and money, and you may not be able to get them because the computers have crashed or malfunctioned.

The picture is even bleaker if you or your loved ones rely on checks from the government. Many experts predict serious problems unless Uncle Sam's computers are fixed. Testifying before Congress last year, Joel C. Williamson, a chief auditor in the U.S. General Accounting Office, warned that "federal agencies are running out of time to prepare for the new millennium," and he urged the government to increase its attention to this problem. Many experts have pointed out that there's simply not enough time between now and December 31, 1999, to reprogram and test the vast numbers of government computers. Chances are excellent that those computers will have serious problems when the new millennium comes.

On the front page of the *Wall Street Journal* (4/22/98), IRS Commissioner Charles Rossotti was quoted as saying: "If we don't fix the century-date problem, we will have a situation scarier than the average disaster movie you see on a Sunday night. Twenty-one months from now, there could be 90 million taxpayers who won't get their refunds, and 95% of the revenue stream of the United States could be jeopardized. [It is] a very, very serious problem."

Think about how this may affect you. If you or your family depends on a government check, and that check is delayed, what will you live on while you wait for the problem to be corrected?

Maybe you're totally independent, and you don't need government assistance. You'd be wrong to assume that you're not affected. There are millions of people around you who depend on the government for welfare of some sort. Imagine the civil unrest that could erupt if they stop getting their support. People have rioted over less, such as a court decision. But imagine a situation in which entire segments of our population are hungry and cold, without money and medical care because the government's computers were unable to issue their checks. If a number of people are suddenly cut off from public assistance, and the grocery shelves in their area are empty, they might come to your neighborhood looking for these things. We could be in the midst of violent revolts that make the 1960s uprisings look like an afternoon tea party.

So, as women we have to ask ourselves: If the year 2000 causes economic disruptions, will we be able to protect our homes and families from desperate looters searching for food and money?

Don't make the mistake of thinking the police will be there to protect you if violence erupts. I have a friend who was in Los Angeles when the riots happened, and she couldn't believe it took so little to ignite such a violent uprising. She was also astonished at how unresponsive the so-called "peace keeping" forces could be. There just wasn't time to mobilize enough police to keep everybody safe. And when a semblance of order was restored, things were not normal. "You can't imagine how scary and surreal it was to go down to the peaceful beach where I walked every day," she told me, "and see National Guardsmen walking around, toting military rifles. I felt as if I were in one of those war-torn, military dictatorships I see on the evening news."

If the Y2K problem is as big a problem as some experts predict (some say the Y2K disruptions will last weeks, months, maybe even years), how long can we expect civil unrest to continue, especially if desperate people believe they have no other options and nothing to lose?

At this point, you may be thinking: "Nobody really knows what's going to happen. What if the computers are fine, and none of them crash?" That would be great . . . but that won't necessarily stop a riot from happening. If even a few people have the perception that something is going wrong, regardless of what the facts really are, they can start a mass panic. When people get stampeded to death at concerts and soccer games, rarely does anyone know what, if anything, actually caused the stampede in the first place. A few people panic, and, before you know it, everybody panics, and pandemonium ensues. It's like someone yelling "FIRE" in a crowded movie theater—people quickly lose their heads in emergencies!

Suppose all the computers work perfectly when the year 2000 comes. Some people might still panic and believe there's going to be a catastrophe, especially if the media, in its typical fashion, smells a sensational story and milks it for all it's worth. Out of fright and uncertainty, people might do things they'd never do under normal conditions, like steal money and food just in case those things become scarce.

Doesn't Being Prepared Make Me Seem "Paranoid"?

If your best friend told you she doesn't carry fire insurance on her house because she doesn't think she'll ever have a fire, you'd probably think she was foolish. Granted, her chances of having a fire are remote, but if that remote chance ever became a reality, it could ruin her financially and emotionally if she had no insurance to help her replace her home and her property. If you've ever gone without medical insurance, you know the anxiety it can bring. Your finances can get wiped out in the blink of an eye with a major hospitalization for one of your kids if you don't have coverage. The psychological benefits of knowing you have a safety net in place, just in case something bad happens, can be an invaluable source of strength for any woman.

I call this the "prepared mindset." It's the willingness to take simple steps to minimize bad consequences if a disaster should ever strike. You probably do it all the time. You wear your seat belt, and you make your kids wear theirs, just in case you have to stop suddenly. You take your vitamins just in case you're not getting enough nutrients in your diet. You double check to make sure you turned the stove off before you leave the house. You put gas in your car before the tank gets too low, just in case you're not near a gas station when you need it.

You still may not be convinced that it's really a problem. That's okay, because what I'm going to recommend about being prepared applies whether you believe in Y2K or not. Being prepared and having a prepared mindset applies to earthquakes, floods, snowstorms, power outages—any kind of disaster, natural or man-made—that could strike. By being prepared for the unlikely event of a disaster, you increase the chances of keeping yourself and your family safe.

Even if you dismiss everything I've said so far about Y2K, I hope you'll stay with me long enough to learn a few simple steps you can take to keep you and your family safe in a range of situations. I hope that at least you'll follow a few of my suggestions so that if you ever find yourself facing a disaster of any kind, you'll increase your chances of getting out of it unscathed.

Can Being Prepared Help in Other Ways?

I know women who have learned the hard way about how being prepared (or not being prepared) can make the difference between tragedy and survival. I can tell you from personal experience that having a prepared mindset can help you, and how not being prepared means you're taking big, unnecessary risks with your own safety and the safety of your family.

Here's what happened to one woman who lived in a "safe" residential neighborhood with a low crime rate and experienced this harrowing incident:

> "One of my deepest fears (and I know it's one shared by many women) is the fear of being attacked. Tragically, I've known more women than I care to count who are rape survivors (some are my close friends). There came a point when I could no longer delude myself that I was somehow immune from becoming a victim. I had a couple of close calls with some very menacing men, and I decided I didn't want to push my luck and risk becoming another crime statistic. So I enrolled in self-defense classes. I wasn't paranoid about being attacked, but I knew that there was a decent chance, based on my experience and the experience of other women, plus the statistics I read, that one day I could be put in a threatening situation. I wanted to be prepared when and if that day came.
>
> "Well, it came one afternoon, in broad daylight, while I was filling my car at a corner gas station. I hadn't bothered to close the driver door, so I was boxed in on three sides between the car, the gas pump, and the open door. I had just taken my

credit card out of the machine and was waiting for the gas to finish pumping when I noticed two young teenagers in baggy, grungy clothing walking toward me. They were wearing caps pulled down low, and the cold, hard way they stared straight ahead gave me the creeps.

"Now, in the old days I would have probably chastised myself for being paranoid and felt guilty about making snap judgments about somebody based only on their looks. But after taking self-defense classes, after learning from veteran cops who'd developed a sixth sense about people and crime, after listening to rape victims who learned the hard way to trust that little voice of warning in their heads, I didn't dismiss my instincts. I trusted what I felt, and what I felt was that these two teenagers were up to no good.

"As they got closer, they suddenly split up. One headed to the side of my car where I was boxed in, and the other went to the other side. I was sure I was being set up for a car-jacking or a hold-up, possibly even a kidnapping. My self-defense training taught me that I had to act quickly, so I kept my eye on the teenager closest to me and walked out into the open, toward him. I didn't want to be trapped with nowhere to run if they were going to try to corner me. Even though I sensed I was in danger and there was very little time to plan, I was able to think about my priorities very clearly. I remember saying to myself, 'They can have the car, but there's no way they're going to get me.' My first concern was to keep myself safe, and worry about the car later.

"I came toward the one teenager with my balance squarely centered, my eyes never leaving his face, and an attitude that I was not going to be a victim. Even if I had to fight to protect myself. That way of carrying myself came from training and practice, from having a prepared mindset. There's no way to fake that kind of an attitude, you have to earn it. And the teenager probably sensed this, because, at the last moment, he turned away to avoid me, and met up with his friend as they left the gas station. I closed my gas tank, grabbed my receipt, got into my car, and locked the doors. As I drove away, I saw him and his friend loitering outside a drugstore next to the gas station. He gave me a vicious glare as I zoomed past him in my car.

"The fact that I avoided becoming a victim wasn't just luck or chance. It was because I had spent time preparing for the possibility that someone might want to hurt me. I learned to recognize and deal with a dangerous situation, and I acted appropriately. Was I paranoid for taking self-defense classes? Some people might say I was. But then again, I managed to avoid getting hurt, and my car wasn't stolen. All because of a prepared mindset."

And then there's the scary story of my friend Christine, who lives in southern California:

"It was 4:31 in the morning that day in January 1994. My husband and I were sound asleep when suddenly it felt as if a huge truck had smashed into our wall. 'Earthquake! Get to the doorway!' he yelled. The floor was shaking so hard I couldn't stand without falling, so I crawled on my hands and knees, groping my way in the darkness. Everything was clattering and creaking, and we could hear the studs in the walls groaning from the shock waves. We prayed our house wouldn't collapse on us.

"At that moment, I wished we'd taken better steps to deal with this emergency. I had never bothered to put together an emergency kit ahead of time, even though I knew we lived in an earthquake zone. But because earthquakes are unpredictable (sometimes they happen only once in several years), it's easy to procrastinate and think, 'Oh, it won't happen for awhile. I have plenty of time.'

"When the shaking stopped, we tried to think about what we needed to do to keep ourselves safe. Because I wasn't prepared, I couldn't think straight. It took me awhile to pull myself together and stop running in circles. I was preoccupied with silly things, like whether I should comb my hair and change my shirt in case we had to go outside. When I was finally able to focus on the essentials, I realized that we needed a lot of time to get basic emergency gear together, and I realized that we lacked essential things. It took me awhile to locate flashlights and candles. We had some water stored, but not enough if we had to survive on it for more than five or six days, and certainly none to spare for cooking, washing or flushing toilets. We had some food, maybe enough for a week, but the electricity was out, and we had no idea for how long. Our stove was electric. If we couldn't cook, the pasta, rice, and dried beans in the pantry wouldn't do us much good. Without electricity, the food in the refrigerator and freezer would eventually spoil. We didn't know if we had hot water. And we didn't know whether our phones still worked.

"After the earthquake, I took a long, hard look at how I took my own safety for granted. Being unprepared was a hard lesson to learn, and I realized that I was taking a huge gamble with my life and the lives of my family members by not storing extra water and food. I vowed I wouldn't make that mistake again. I hope other people won't make that mistake, either."

I've spent a lot of time telling you about computers, the Y2K problem and harrowing accounts of two friends' experiences (one with a near car-jacking and another with an earthquake). The point of all this isn't to make you panic or get depressed, just as the weather forecaster who tells you about an incoming hurricane isn't trying to make you panic. The point is to make you aware of what's happening so you can take steps to keep your family safe and secure.

It would be easy for you to dismiss what you've read and say, "Nobody knows for sure what will happen, so I'll just ignore it and hope somebody will take care of it." However, with this attitude, you're taking a big risk with your family's security.

If a disaster strikes, and your children want to know why you can't buy the food and necessities they need, or why there are so many problems getting money out of the bank, or why the house is so cold, will you be able to look into their faces and say, "Because I didn't want to take the necessary steps to prepare for it"?

It doesn't matter who's right about the Y2K problem. It doesn't matter whether you think the worst thing that will happen is your

VCR's programming might get messed up, or whether you think the Y2K problem will plunge our society into a major upheaval. *What matters is that you take steps to prepare now for something you can see coming.* You'll give yourself a tremendous sense of relief knowing you took steps to keep your family safe. Then you won't have to lose sleep as the date gets closer. You can rest assured you've done whatever you could to weather the uncertainty.

What if your friends or family think you're paranoid for taking the precautions I've outlined below? Think of it this way: You probably have fire insurance, right? Are you "paranoid" that your house is going to burn down? Of course not. You want to be prepared just in case. And you'd probably think anyone who accused you of being paranoid for having fire insurance was crazy and irresponsible.

It's the same with preparing for other possible emergencies. You have nothing to lose by having emergency supplies. And if disaster doesn't strike, then all the better for you. At least you were prepared. Besides, you don't have to tell anyone you're making preparations, just as you don't have to share information about what kind of insurance you carry.

How Can I Keep My Family Safe in the Event of a Disaster?

Here's where my perspective as a woman comes in. I've read a lot of stuff on preparing for the Y2K problem. No disrespect intended, but much of it is written by men who seem to love the idea of slipping into some old army fatigues and redecorating the garage in "early camouflage" so they can act out their Rambo fantasies.

I have a number of good women friends who've spent lots of time roughing it with Mother Nature, camping in remote areas that were only accessible by canoe. On wilderness treks, they've gotten used to going without a decent hairstyle and shaved legs, not to mention mirrors, makeup and baths. They don't mind wearing the same clothes for many days straight, with their only accessories being the leaves and bugs that happen to land on them.

It's just that that's not me! Personally, I hate olive green, and visiting Army/Navy surplus stores can be a drab experience indeed. Don't get me wrong, I'm no "pampered housewife." It's just that when I'm in civilization, I like things to be, well, civilized. And when it comes to my home, I could make Martha Stewart look uncouth.

For example, I refuse to mount the fire extinguisher on the wall because it would ruin the decor of the kitchen (my color scheme isn't fire engine red!). Instead, I discreetly tuck it into a corner, out of sight, but still accessible. In my opinion, just because you're making preparations to keep your family safe in the event of an upheaval doesn't mean your house has to look like an army bunker. In fact, some of my suggestions may even enhance your standard of living, if, for instance, you and your husband find yourselves home some cold night with plenty of firewood, warm sleeping bags, and lots of pretty candles . . .

The trick here is balance! (Sometimes I hate that word!) You don't have to turn your home into a military camp. Yet, at the same time, having what you need in an emergency is worth doing some rearranging to make sure you have all the things you need for your family's safety, protection and comfort.

Chapter 1:
Y2K Basics

1. Dear Karen: I feel stupid asking this, but what exactly is the Y2K problem?

Here's the way I understand it as a "non-techie" person. Basically, the year 2000 problem (also know as Y2K—Y for year and 2K for 2000) is about whether computers, especially old computers, will be able to recognize a date change.

When the programmers of the 1950s and 1960s were designing computer software, "memory" was very expensive, and "storage" was as big as a room. To save money (a management issue) and space they just shaved the first two digits off the year, so 1972 would be just 72. Everybody, including the computer, knew it was the year 1972. The programmers figured that by the year 2000 (which seemed like a million years away) all their equipment would be obsolete and everybody would be using something fancy by then.

Well, they were partially correct. We do have some very fancy and cheap computers nowadays, and many of them are designed to read the year 2000. But the kicker is that not all of our computers are fancy . . . some of those big old "mainframe" computers are still around, plugging away just exactly as they did 30 or 40 years ago.

Because computers are relatively expensive machines (and they used to be extremely expensive years ago), many companies (and in particular the government) didn't want to throw out their expensive old computers and buy expensive new ones. So they simply tinkered and patched the old mainframes to accept new programs. But the old computers are still basically old computers, with some additions. It's kind of like taking an old car and giving it a new paint job and new license plates. It may have updated features, but basically it's still an old car and it performs like one.

When the first day of the year 2000 comes, it will go into most computers as 1/1/00. So, many computers will think it's the year 1900, not the year 2000, and any calculations having to do with the date will be wrong. Some computers may stop working (in technical terms, they'll "crash"), or they may just get really confused about what day it is and spew out incorrect information.

Let me take it a step further. When the early programmers wrote the code (the information that tells the computer what it's supposed to do), they wrote it in specific "languages." The only problem is, there were lots of different languages and dialects. In looking at those languages today, it's like reading old Egyptian hieroglyphics—you have to figure out what the hieroglyphics are.

To make matters more complicated, there were many programmers writing in "hieroglyphics," and, while two pictures may not have looked the same, both would communicate and work fine when they were written.

The same thing is basically true when programmers were writing lines of code. Each one was a little different, and most of them were custom made. So today, when trying to figure out which lines of code have a "date" problem, programmers have to go in and read each line of code one by one. Instead of being able to say, "Find the word 'date' and go in and change it to four characters instead of two," they have to look at each line to see what it says. One line may use the word "time," another "date," another "birthday," while another may use "clock." There are all kinds of words that could have been used. You have to go in and decipher the language for each individual program and figure out what the key word is that affects the date.

Unfortunately, since each line is possibly different you can't just look at the whole program. You have to look at each line within each program, so we are talking about billions and billions of lines of code.

Granted, there are computer programs that will help go in and find the line, but, in essence, somebody with some kind of a brain has to figure out what the word is that each individual programmer may have used to describe the "date." Even within programs and lines of code, different programmers would work on different sections of it, so there's not even consistency within the section. So if I worked on this particular part of the program, and you worked on that particular part of the program, we might be using a little bit different language, a little bit different wording. We'd get the same outcome, but we might have reached that outcome using different languages.

On top of that, there are many different ways to write the date in numbers. For example, when I write my birth date, I usually write it as 7/26/54. But there are many ways to write it: 07/26/54, 26/07/54, 1954/07/26, 1954/26/07, Jul/26/54, and the list goes on.

Everything was done to save space and money. So what happens is, now there's this enormous big deal because the "hieroglyphics" language they wrote is an antiquated language. And, not thinking they'd ever need to know the languages or the programs, nobody kept records to go back and check. Nobody knows for sure what's buried in a lot of computer programs (especially those behemoth mainframes used by the federal and state governments).

Then to make today's situation more "challenging," many of those original programmers have either retired (and no amount of money can pry them away from the ole fishin' hole), or they've passed on to that big computer heaven in the sky. The old computer languages (like COBOL) haven't been taught except as foundations in years, and the modern-day technology whiz kids aren't familiar with those ancient computer languages. Those few programmers who do know the languages are commanding top dollar to fix the problem, but there aren't many of them to go around.

If that isn't complicated enough, there is another issue involving computer dates, and that is in "embedded chips." If you're not familiar at all with computers, a crude analogy for understanding the difference between "hardware" and "software" is a player piano. As you know, player pianos have rolls of paper in them with little holes that cause particular keys on the piano to play music, without the need of a human being to actually depress the keys.

So, the roll of paper in the player piano is roughly analogous to the software of a computer. The insides of the piano—the mallets and the metal strings—are kind of like the hardware of a computer.

Suppose you put a roll of music in a player piano that has holes punched in the wrong places. When the piano plays, it will strike wrong notes because the roll of music—its "software"—was faulty. Suppose the roll of music you install is perfect, but the piano still plays wrong notes. You look inside the instrument, and you find that some of the strings inside are too loose or too tight, and some mallets are missing. In this case, the "hardware" of the piano is messed up, which explains why it plays music badly.

Up to this point, we've been talking about a computer's software, the program that tells the computer what to do. Now we turn to the hardware, the "brains" of the computer. A crucial component of a computer's hardware is its microchips. A computer microchip is a tiny component with incredibly large amounts of information on it given its size relative to the amount of information it can hold—progress in computers these days is measured by how little the chip is compared to the amount of information it holds. In fact, you may have seen the Intel commercials on TV where the camera winds its way through the guts of the computer, to show you that the chip is buried deep in the computer. It's like a roll of music that has not just a few hundred notes, but millions and millions of notes.

Many of those microchips (or "chips" for short) have dates in them. "Embedded" means the chip is part of the hardware. Suppose someone gave you a loaf of raisin bread. If you wanted to remove the raisins, you'd have to go through each slice bit by bit to remove them. It's the same thing with the microchips: the date chips are embedded in hardware like raisins in the bread.

Those microchips are literally in everything, and they are everywhere. They're in microwaves and grocery store scanners and automobiles and tons of things we use in our lives every day.

Are they all going to be screwy with the date change?

No . . . it's just that we don't know which ones will work and which ones won't!

Then, just to add insult to injury, the data from a computer that's okay ("2000-compliant") can essentially get "infected" by the data from a computer that's got date problems (non-compliant). This means that if my business has its computers all brand new and Y2K-compliant, and my computer "talks" to another computer by modem, my computer is at risk for getting major problems.

Again, this doesn't mean that when the clock strikes midnight of 1999, ALL computers are going to stop. It's actually worse. Some computers may keep running but give incorrect information!

So how bad is that? Well, let's look at what typically happens on a home computer today. Many computers at home are used for personal finances (plus lots of games for the kids!). Today, if I'm using Quicken to keep my checkbook balanced (and provided that I've entered the numbers correctly), I assume that Quicken's math calculations are right. I know that if I added up a column of numbers on a sheet of paper (with no calculator!) and Quicken added those same numbers, we should come up with the same total. But if my total is different, well . . . there's more than a good chance I'm wrong!

But what happens if my computer becomes infected? How would I know whether Quicken's addition or mine was correct? Or the bank's records or mine are correct? Or the government's Social Security records or mine are correct? Remember, computers can't think and don't think.

Another example of how computers can't think is the beloved "spell check" function on the computer. Now, I don't want to say I'm a bad speller . . . it's just that it's so boring to spell a word the same way twice!

When I type a letter to a friend on my computer and the spell checker says a word is spelled wrong, I trust the computer's spelling. But occasionally, I'll intend to write a word like "guest" but hit the wrong key and spell "quest" instead. The computer doesn't see the word is spelled wrong since there is a word "quest." This actually happened to me one time when I sent a letter out to people for a fund raising banquet. I didn't proofread my letter, thinking that the spell check would have caught any mistakes. I invited a large number of people to be my quest at the banquet! I have to admit, I took a fair amount of teasing for quite some time!

Right now our confidence in the accuracy of our computers is pretty high. But what would happen if even a small percentage of computers started giving bad information?

The typical response I get from most women I talk to about the year 2000 problem goes something like this: "It won't affect me personally. Besides, someone will take care of it sooner or later." As I said, this was my response for many months until I began to research and study the situation in more depth. After months of research and analysis, I noticed that everybody who knows anything about Y2K or writes about it says the same thing: It's definitely a problem for each and every one of us. The only disagreement is over how big and widespread the problem will be when the new millennium comes.

Can't the problem be fixed?

The answer is yes! Technically, it's easy to fix. The problem is that it's so time-consuming to fix each line of code, and there are so many billions of lines of code to be fixed *that there just isn't enough time to get it all fixed before the deadline of December 31, 1999.*

It's like needing to change all the light bulbs in Las Vegas. Sure it can be done, but the time it would take to change each light bulb by hand is astronomical!

If everything isn't fixed and tested, problems will occur all at the same time (a cumulative effect). Then, if non-compliant computers start contaminating clean computers (the ripple effect), you have the possibility of one big ugly mess! It's like leaving the ball park in the last two minutes of the game in order to beat the traffic. If the score is close, and you wait until the end of the game to leave, you know you'll be sitting in a traffic jam of cars trying to get out of the parking lot, all at the same time!

(In fact, some people predict that the date change problem will come months sooner than December 31, 1999. For example, many municipalities begin their fiscal years in April so April of 1999 should be indicative of what might happen. Another date to look for is September 9, 1999. In some computer programs, nines are read as a signal to stop. So, some computers might interpret 9/9/99 as a signal that they should shut down their programs.)

Personally, I'm not a pessimist, and I don't think the world is coming to an end. But the world as we know it may be coming to an end. Just as there is an aftermath from a hurricane or tornado, I do think there will be major inconveniences. I say this because I've read a lot about this subject and talked with many experts. I believe that everyone, particularly women, needs to prepare for these inconveniences and upheavals now.

I'm talking about the same kind of inconveniences that could befall you if there were a natural disaster, such as an earthquake, tornado, hurricane or ice storm. And the steps I'll recommend later for dealing with such disasters will make your life easier should something unexpected occur. Best of all, if you follow even just a few of the simple steps I'll share with you, you'll gain valuable peace of mind. You won't have to be up nights worrying about the future or losing your head if those around you start to panic when the century rolls over.

Unlike an earthquake or a flood, the Y2K problem is predictable. There are small, inexpensive things you can start doing now to ensure that you and your family can look forward to New Year's Eve 1999 with anticipation, not dread. If you take action now you won't have to fear it, and you can minimize its effects on your life.

2. Dear Karen: Why doesn't somebody just fix it?

Unfortunately, the problem has turned out to be too huge to accomplish in the little time we have left. Why? Because nobody kept track of all the little nooks and crannies where the date is encoded into a computer's programming. If you've ever seen an actual computer program—not the glossy box you buy in the computer store, but the weird-looking gibberish that actually commands the computer to do its job—then you know that it can take several pages of this gibberish just to tell your computer to perform a simple function such as erase a line of text or draw a green circle. Finding all the date-sensitive lines buried amidst those piles and piles of programming pages could take years. To make matters worse, some computers and computerized machines have actual chips inside them that are date-sensitive, and those chips will have to be physically replaced by a computer technician. It's a mess. Although lots of folks are working feverishly on it now, to the tune of billions of dollars, it appears that many businesses and government departments procrastinated so long that they simply won't be finished in time. The next millennium is coming, whether we're ready or not.

3. Dear Karen: Isn't this a problem only for people who rely heavily on computers?

Unless you live in a cave, this problem could affect you a great deal, even if you don't own a computer. Why? Because just about every service you take for granted is run by computer.

In the worst-case scenario, when their non-compliant computers have Y2K problems, many of those services will abruptly shut down or begin making serious errors. In the best-case scenario, the next millennium will ring in just like any other new year (but just about everybody agrees that's a fantasy). The odds are, reality will be somewhere in between those two extremes, and how severely it will hit us won't be known until we're smack dab in the middle of it.

The Power Grid Problem

By the way, there's another reason to be prepared to take care of yourself without public utilities. No matter where you live, chances are you've had at least some experience with power outages and isolation due to high winds, earthquakes, floods, lightning strikes, tornadoes, hurricanes or ice storms. I have friends who kept themselves quite comfortable for two weeks without electricity, heat, and phone after a north Idaho ice storm—all because they were well-prepared. With sub-zero temperatures and roads hopelessly blocked, they stayed warm and well-fed, their pets were cozy and happy, and although in retrospect it was a huge inconvenience, they look back on their "ice storm" experience as a great family adventure. Had they not been prepared, it might have created an entirely different sort of memory.

4. Dear Karen: So, what services are vulnerable to shutdown?

Anything that involves computers in some way, including any or all of the following: public utilities such as electricity, natural gas (because of computer-driven and/or electric switches in the gas line), telephone (including cellular, if the signal is routed through ground offices); garbage pickup; running water (because it takes electricity to run the pumps); city sewers (those requiring electricity to move, store, and/or treat the effluent); public transportation; cargo transport (which is vital to keeping shelves stocked in grocery stores, hardware stores, pet stores, farm and feed stores, hunting and fishing shops, and so on); postal and parcel delivery; medical facilities (including laboratory services, kidney dialysis, all diagnostic imaging services such as x-ray, CAT scans and MRI, computer-driven IV systems, the blood bank, high-tech diagnostic and treatment equipment, ambulance and life-flight dispatch as well as communication en route); all businesses that require computers for records, communications, and/or production; Social Security payments; Medicare and Medicaid as well as private insurance; your investment portfolios; the banking system (including account records, ATM machines, and date-linked interest compounding); and any free-standing devices that contain date-sensitive programming or hardware (some people have suggested that such devices might include automobiles, pacemakers, commercial airlines and air-traffic control, cameras, etc.).

5. Dear Karen: I heard that there are embedded computer chips in all sorts of things that could mean disaster if they shut down, such as cardiac pacemakers, car engines, commercial airplanes, air traffic control, medical devices in hospitals, and so forth. Should I be worried? I have a pacemaker, but I've not received any recall notices for "fixing" its internal computer. I have plans to fly somewhere for a vacation around Y2K time. Should I cancel my tickets?

I've asked several folks who sell and/or maintain medical

devices about the pacemaker question, and everybody has given me the same answer: The pacemaker does contain a "timing device," but it does not care what year it is. Therefore, it is not "date-sensitive." If I had a pacemaker inside me, however, I might want more of a guarantee. If you want something in writing, you can engage in a little medical activism by either calling your primary care physician or the surgeon who implanted the pacemaker, or getting someone to do it for you. Ask for the name and telephone number of the manufacturer of your pacemaker (or, at least, the name and number of the distributor that sold it to the hospital). If you're persistent, you'll eventually be put in touch with someone who can tell you, in no uncertain terms, whether your concerns are legitimate, and put it in writing for you. If you aren't able to get that sort of assurance yourself, you may be better able to plow through to the right person if you engage an attorney to make the calls for you. Just about everybody knows at least one attorney—perhaps now's the time to ask for a favor.

As far as automobiles are concerned, it took some doing for me to find somebody who was both computer-knowledgeable and auto mechanics-knowledgeable at the same time. When I finally did find such a person, he told me that although there are several computer chips embedded in modern engines, the only date-sensitive chip in most automobiles is the diagnostic computer that stores information about engine misbehavior. In other words, it's the computer that the mechanic at say, a GM dealership, plugs into his big computer in the garage, to tell him whether your engine has been operating properly since your last checkup. A breakdown may not affect the way your car runs, but it might affect the mechanic's ability to diagnose any problems your car might be experiencing. Rather than fix all the chips embedded in the cars, the automakers probably will focus their efforts on the diagnostic machines in the garage. So, the consensus at this point is your cars and trucks probably will run just fine. (However, fuel for your car or truck may be another story!)

At publication time, the word around Washington and the FAA office was that air traffic may well be affected, at least in terms of air traffic control. Some spokespersons are saying it's not a prob-

lem—the air traffic controllers can always "switch to manual"—
but if that's what they have to do, there will need to be a 20%
reduction in flights in order to accommodate the increased confusion, and bad weather (especially the kind that affects visibility)
will be more likely to cause flight delays, cancellations, or diver-
sions to other airports. So, the problem may amount to safety and
lots more than inconvenience.

I also would be surprised if the airlines will actually allow
planes to fly over the millennium change because of insurance
coverage issues. My guess is that since loss related to Y2K problems is not covered under insurance coverage, airlines are not
going to want to take the chance and risk the liability until they
are for sure that it is safe.

Although there were lots of opinions, nobody could say with
any degree of certainty that the planes would fly normally at Y2K,
and in all likelihood nobody knows for sure. Modern-day airplanes are complicated behemoths. I won't tell you what to do
about your travel plans, but I will tell you that I intend to stay
home during the last few days of 1999 and a few days into 2000,
just to be on the safe side.

Regarding hospital equipment and other medical devices, the
Food & Drug Administration (FDA) is collecting compliance
information from medical device manufacturers and has set up a
database for people who have questions about this or that specific
device. The trouble is, how can you be certain whether to believe
responses of "everything will be fine" from a spokesperson from a
company that makes, for example, a kidney dialysis machine? It
seems logical that, although hospitals are a veritable sea of embedded computer chips, many things will run normally if they don't
operate with embedded chips. Again, the problem is we don't
know where many of those chips are going to turn up until after
the fact.

6. Dear Karen: If the worst-case scenario happens, how long will it last? How long should I prepare for?

To answer your second question, you need to take stock of
your individual needs, and ask yourself what level of preparedness

will give you peace of mind. I call this your "grace period." For the sake of illustration, many folks feel comfortable if they're prepared for a grace period of six months—in other words, they believe that any community breakdown that occurs will be adequately resolved in that space of time. Some people are satisfied with less, some with more. (Some churches encourage their members to be prepared to hunker down and live, completely self-sufficiently, for two whole years.)

I know it sounds like I'm dodging your first question, and in a sense, I am. Here's why: The degree to which today's world depends on computers is a completely new experience for our civilization. Thirty years ago, we didn't even have drive-through banking, let alone ATM machines, satellite TV, cellular telephones, and a computer-driven government. Today, our civilization is pretty much built on a foundation of computers, and because we've never experienced a situation where all (or many) computers shut down or malfunction simultaneously, nobody really knows how big a mess it'll be, how long it'll last, and how hard it'll be to clean up.

So, all you can do is come up with a solution based on a combination of your practical nature, your faith, and what's required to give you a feeling of security. There's no wrong answer here—if one week's, or one month's, or six months', or two years' worth of preparation is what it takes to help you feel secure, then that's what you have to do. My position is that it is better to be safe than sorry.

7. Dear Karen: What frightens me the most is that I don't think our governments around the world are being straight with us about what they already know is going to fail and things that will fail earlier than December 1999. Do we have as much time as we think?

The issue of time is one of the biggest concerns regarding Y2K. In fact, maybe it's just me, but it feels like time is flying faster! One of the things most people agree on is that there isn't enough time to fix all the problems before New Year's Eve of 1999. Yet something that has me disturbed is, many people believe that problems won't happen until December 31, 1999. In fact, I believe there will be many times before then that may have problems associated with Y2K. When and if that happens, we'll be able to see what kind of impact those problems will have.

One of the major dates to watch for worldwide is what happens when the new fiscal year begins. April will be a very telling time (and not just April 15th!) when we will see how things unfold for many big cities and countries.

When looking at dates in April, one day in particular that has many people wondering about is when we hit the 99th day of the 99th year. The reason this is an issue is that some programs were written to recognize 9999 to mean stop or end of program. This is a problem for files that may be open and would be closed by the computer or it may cause active files to become inactive. Now, one would think that this wouldn't be a problem because the date should really be written 09/09/99. But remember, computers can't think, and it all depends on how the code was written.

What I recommend is that you watch carefully what is going on beginning in January. Depending on what you see, you may want to speed up your efforts to be prepared, but, nevertheless, the point is to keep watch as you make your plans.

Here are some key dates:

- January 1, 1999: Start of Calendar Year 1999.
- January 1, 1999: Transition to the Euro begins within continental Europe. The transition period goes through December 31, 2002.
- January 1, 1999: Beginning of annual renewal dates for insurance policies
- January 2, 1999: The first day of work in 1999.
- March 7, 1999: 300 days until 1/1/2000.
- March 19, 1999: Triple Witching Day on Wall Street, very heavy volume of stock trading.
- March 31, 1999: The target date for all branches of the federal government to be running remediated code.
- March 31, 1999: The target date given by telecommunica-

tions industry to receive year 2000 fixes from their software vendors.

● March 31, 1999: The target date for banks to be compliant or they are dropped from Fannie Mae (national pools of government guaranteed mortgage funds).

● March 31, 1999: New SEC rules: all publicly traded companies each quarter must disclose their "state of readiness," including what proportion of their hardware has been tested. Companies must divulge historical and estimated costs directly related to fixing Y2K problems.

● April 1, 1999: Beginning of 1999-2000 fiscal year for Japan, Canada, and New York State.

● April 1, 1999: Start of fiscal year 1999 in Japan.

● April 6, 1999: Start of Fiscal Year 2000 in the United Kingdom.

● April 9, 1999: 99th day of 1999, recorded as 99/99 on some systems. Mimics a system halt command on many systems.

● April 20, 1999: 255 days until 1/1/2000. "255" is the highest number in one byte. This may cause some programs to crash. (256 is 2 raised to the 8th power minus 1.)

● June 15, 1999: 200 days until 1/1/2000. Programs that calculate ahead by 200 days may crash on this day.

● June 18, 1999: Triple Witching Day on Wall Street, very heavy volume of stock trading.

● June 30, 1999: New SEC rules: all publicly traded companies each quarter must disclose their "state of readiness," including what proportion of their hardware has been tested. Companies must divulge historical and estimated costs directly related to fixing Y2K problems. Companies need to include a description of their most likely worst-case scenarios. Companies must detail how they are preparing to handle their worst-case scenarios.

● July 1, 1999: Start of Fiscal Year 2000 in 46 of the 50 states and Australia. Six-month projections fail unless the code is fully year 2000 compliant.

● July 1, 1999: The deadline for nuclear power plants to prove compliance or be shut down by the NRC.

● August 22, 1999: G.P.S. (Global Positioning Satellite)

rollover week. Since many (most?) devices use the G.P.S. time signal for synchronization, there is a possibility of failures on this day as well, even though this isn't a Y2K problem. (Actual point of failure is a few seconds before midnight August 21, but the effects will be noticed on August 22.)

● September 1, 1999: Start of Fiscal Year 2000 in Texas.

● September 9, 1999: 9/9/99 used as special key by lots of programmers. Mimics a system halt command on many systems.

● September 17, 1999: Triple Witching Day on Wall Street, very heavy volume of stock trading. Another possible date for a stock market crash.

● September 23, 1999: 100 days until 1/1/2000.

● September 24, 1999: 99 days until 1/1/2000.

● September 30, 1999: New SEC rules: all publicly traded companies each quarter must disclose their "state of readiness," including what proportion of their hardware has been tested. Companies must divulge historical and estimated costs directly related to fixing Y2K problems. Companies need to include a description of their most likely worst-case scenarios. Companies must detail how they are preparing to handle their worst-case scenarios.

● October 1, 1999: Start of Fiscal Year 2000 for the Federal Government, Alabama, and Michigan. Three-month projections may fail.

● October 3, 1999: 90 days until 1/1/2000.

● November 2, 1999: 60 days until 1/1/2000.

● November 17, 1999: Peak of Leonid meteor storm. Expect some damage to communications and navigation satellites.

● December 1, 1999: One-month projections fail.

● December 2, 1999: 30 days until 1/1/2000.

● December 17, 1999: Triple Witching Day on Wall Street, very heavy volume of stock trading.

● December 21, 1999: Full moon on the day of the winter equinox.

● December 23, 1999: Last workday of 1999 for those who have the week of Christmas and New Year's off.

● December 31, 1999: New Year's Eve of the Millennium

Change. Tapes and mass storage devices marked "expire on 12/31/99" meant as "keep indefinitely" are automatically purged.

● January 1, 2000: The single biggest day for computer failures. Expect embedded chip failures as well. The first day after "1999/99/99," so support for some software may cease.

● January 1, 2000: Approximate peak of sunspot 13-year cycle. It may be difficult to figure out what is Y2K and what is sunspot problems.

● January 3, 2000: The first regular business day (Monday) in the year 2000 in the U.S.

● January 4, 2000: The first regular business day (Tuesday) in the year 2000 in the U.K.

● January 10, 2000: First date that requires 7 digits: 1/10/2000.

● January 31, 2000: First end-of-month in the year 2000.

● February, 2000: New Hampshire primary.

● February 29, 2000: Many systems will forget about the leap year day. Since 2000 is divisible by 400, there is a leap year in 2000. While this may sound obscure, it can be the cause of massive computer failures if computers which are in contact with each other do not agree on what day it is.

● March 1, 2000: It is reported that most Digital PDP-8 computers will not boot from this day on. Some leap year errors will start to show up.

● March 3, 2000: If software is not programmed for leap year correctly, this is the first Friday when the computer thinks it is Saturday. School bells may fail to operate, bank vaults may fail to open.

● March 31, 2000: First end-of-quarter in the year 2000.

● April 1, 2000: Start of Fiscal Year 2000 in Japan.

● October 10, 2000: First date that requires 8 digits: 10/10/2000.

● December 31, 2000: First end-of-year in the year 2000.

● January 1, 2001: The official start of the third millennium and the twenty-first century.

● January 1, 2001: Some versions of Microsoft Windows correct year 2000 problems, but fail in 2001. A new round

of personal computer failures.
● February 29, 2001: This date does not exist.
● September 8, 2001: The Unix end-of-file problem. This date is represented by 999,999,999, which is the same number that some Unix applications use to denote the end of a file.
● January 1, 2002: (Burroughs) Unisys A series system date is reported to fail.
● January 1, 2003: Transition to the Euro is completed in continental Europe.

But remember, the reason I'm telling you this is not for you to panic and get freaked out! It is to let you know that, just like predicting the weather, there are sometimes indicators or warnings that happen before the storm hits that help you to protect yourself and your family. These are sort of like storm warnings. (In Texas, we have tornado warnings and watches, and I usually get them confused! But I know one means conditions are ripe for a tornado and the other means a tornado has been spotted and to take appropriate measures.)

8. Dear Karen: I was just wondering why the mainstream media has not addressed this issue in depth. Are they afraid that it would cause an economic and social panic?

Great questions! On June 2, 1997, *Newsweek* magazine ran an article entitled, "The Day the World Shuts Down." Now that wasn't June 1998, but June 1997. It detailed and outlined what probable problems Y2K could cause and the profound ramifications on our society. What was the response to this article? Basically nothing! A few people began to see the implications of Y2K but for all intents and purposes, absolutely nothing happened. There are three reasons why I think nobody responded.

1) It was too "early," meaning Y2K still seemed too far away. If I told you today that you should start being concerned about what was going to happen in the year 2003, would you do anything today? Probably not. There wasn't much public response until June of 1998—the 18-month mark. Then it seemed as if the millennium change was just around the corner.

2) We are fairly used to sensationalism in the media. We don't pay much attention to headlines these days because they all sort of blend together after awhile. I remember my favorite headline a few years ago that was on a tabloid magazine next to the checkout counter at the grocery store. It read, "New Diet Soap Washes Away Fat." It didn't seem believable, so I ignored it. (I only wished that it were true!)

3) We believe everything will have a "happily ever after" Hollywood ending. It seems everyone these days is comparing Y2K to *Titanic*. The movie *Titanic* was a blockbuster hit and everyone can clearly and graphically see the consequences of lack of planning and foresight. But my point in looking at the movie, one that is most absurd to me and one that the American public has overlooked, is that *Titanic* has a happy ending. If you saw it (and the ticket sales demonstrate that many, many people have seen it) the two main characters, Jack and Rose, are surrealistically reunited at the end of the movie. She waltzes into his waiting arms, they kiss, and you assume they live happily every after (although the fact that they are dead doesn't seem to play into the emotion of the final scene). My point is that Hollywood has put its spin on the story, and we are able to leave the theater feeling good rather than feeling the tragic loss of the many deaths. Is it any wonder we don't think anything bad is going to happen?

All this is to say that it doesn't surprise me that nobody has paid all that much attention to Y2K. So, where does that leave us? With very little time left to get the word out.

9. Dear Karen: I know that Y2K is primarily a big computer problem. Is it safe to assume that my home computer is okay?

No! It is not safe to assume that your home computer is okay. Now, even if you don't use a computer for anything but email, please don't stop reading here because you think this doesn't pertain to you. Hang in there with me, because some of this information is also useful in helping other people to understand the Y2K problem.

I recently picked up a copy of *PC Magazine*, not because it is a magazine that I normally read, but because it had a huge headline that said, *"The Year 2000 Crisis: What You Need to Do to Protect Yourself from the Millennium Bug."*

It made me realize that one of the things I haven't really covered up to this point is how Y2K will affect home computers.

So here's my confession: I haven't taken the time to test my home computer or laptop yet to see if they are Y2K compliant! As it is, there doesn't seem to be enough hours in the day to get everything done, and I figured I had plenty of time to check them out. And for the most part, I think of Y2K as a BIG problem globally and one that affects my home. But I hadn't really paid any attention to my PC (personal computer). Big mistake!

If you love all the computer-techie stuff, I'd recommend that you find a copy of the October 6, 1998, issue of *PC Magazine* (and if you have men in your life who are still discounting Y2K, this is a great issue to give to them). But for those of you who don't want to try and find it, I'm going to give you the highlights and quote a number of things from this issue.

Editor-in-Chief Michael Miller has a list of five myths about Y2K:

1. The year 2000 problem affects only mainframes.

He says, "I wish that were true, but it's not; PCs have the Y2K problem as well. In fact, the problem has nothing to do with the type of computer—only with the programmers' desire to store dates in two digits instead of four."

2. The problem will occur at midnight on 1/1/00.

"If only it were that simple! . . . Some problems will occur even earlier. September 9,1999, is a date that many people worry about, because some programmers used 9/9/99 to indicate an invalid date field. Others worry about the 99th day of 1999 (April 9,1999).

3. The world will end as we know it on 1/1/00.

"Some people think that everything electronic will stop

working forever that morning. Large businesses are well aware of the problem and have every incentive to fix the big problems before then." [KA: I don't think the world will end either, but I think it will be really messed up!]

4. The problems are well-known.

"Even though the basic Y2K problem is well-understood, the difficulty is finding all the places where dates show up. Two-digit date codes were used in all kinds of places on all kinds of systems."

5. Y2K is a technical problem.

"Certainly, there are technical problems that must be addressed, but the legal, public relations, and political issues are just as important. On the legal front, some claim that software developers should be legally responsible for making sure every version of software ever sold is Y2K-ready. Politically, my biggest concern is with government computers. Politicians don't want to spend money that is as invisible as fixing lines of code. PR-wise, I expect you'll start seeing a lot more scare stories about how planes will fall from the sky [KA: Personally, I don't think they'll be flying during that time.] and power will fail everywhere because of the Y2K problem. My guess is that on the actual day there will be a few problems, particularly with government systems. It won't be painless, but we will get through it."

Article Highlights: *PC Things You Need to Think About:*

"One of the enduring myths about Y2K is that the problems are all mainframe—and minicomputer-related; that PC hardware and software that didn't exist in those bad old COBOL [computer programming language] days are immune. Wrong, wrong, wrong. PC problems may be secondary to the huge problems with other hardware and software but are nonetheless present, critical and daunting to solve.

"These problems can show up in your systems' internal hardware clocks, in OSs [operating systems like Windows], and in software programs [like Excel]. They are most insidious in some spreadsheets, data bases, and files that you may have built and customized for yourself over the years and which now may have date-calculation problems when they hit the year 2000 rollover.

"It's disconcerting to discover that some PCs manufactured as recently as 1997 have Y2K-noncompliant BIOSs . . . No one should assume a given PC or other computer hardware is okay without running validation tests and seeking compliance information on that specific model from its manufacturer.

"As we get closer to the millennium, Y2K will start to affect more and more non-compliant systems that use expiration dates or that use dates for forecasting. Software and computations that are date-sensitive can fail outright or produce erroneous results. [KA: Don't miss this one, ladies. These guys just said unless it gets fixed, your computer could make huge mistakes!] Some problems will go undiscovered until it's too late and data is already corrupted. Seemingly small problems with a critical piece of equipment or application can bring a business to its knees." [KA: This is really important for those of you who have home-based businesses like me.]

The bottom line is that you have to check out your hardware, your OS (operating system) and individual software. Download one of the utilities at *PC Magazine's* Y2K Utilities at http://www.zdnet.com/pcmag/pctech/download/swcol.y2k.html to test your system for Year 2000 compliance.

Now here's the scary part. Remember up in myth #5 where the editor says ". . . My guess is that on the actual day there will be a few problems, particularly with government systems. It won't be painless, but we will get through it." Here's what Jim Seymour says in his piece "My Biggest Worry" on the last page of the Y2K article. "I'm betting on—against, that is—the power industry. I award that booby prize for two reasons, and in the language of logicians, both reasons meet the 'necessary and sufficient' test. That is, either on its own would be plenty cause for worry, but the combination of the two looks especially bad.

"First, the electric-power industry has an enormous amount of work to do, and it is doing a terrible job of getting ready for Y2K.

"Second, no matter the remediation work on systems in every other industry—getting elevators working, fixing telecom switches, updating thousands or millions of PC BIOSs—if there's no electrical power in your area for an extended period, you're in deep trouble.

"The power industry's big problem lies in embedded systems, which are in fact, part of everyone's Y2K problem. 'Embedded systems' is shorthand for the billions of programmed micro-processors (programmable logic controllers, or PLCs) hidden inside nearly every piece of sophisticated equipment in use today. Your car has hundreds; power plants have many thousands—or more.

"All PLCs contain software code, which is almost always impenetrable to the people who own and operate the systems. Worse for the companies that produced those PLCs, that code is often badly documented—if at all.

"So utilities have the job of tracking down all these PLCs, though the companies have no idea how may PLCs there are, where they are, or what precise role they play in process control. They must then test each one for Y2K compliance. If the embedded systems are not Y2K compliant and are not specifically upgradeable, the whole piece of machinery has to be replaced. Not only can that be a crushing and expensive burden, but many of these machines must be ordered years in advance." Get the picture? Given all that they have to do, the power companies must have made a good start on this, working on Y2K problems for years, right?

"In January, the Public Utilities Company of Texas surveyed the state's 176 generation and distribution companies on their Y2K readiness. Only 44 percent responded. None were yet compliant, and none had any clear idea when they would be. Among Texas electric co-ops, only 18 percent had written plans for Y2K preparations, and 24 percent said they hadn't yet begun planning. So the PUC, which has absolute regulatory control over these agencies, roared back with a list of recommendations, including 'continuing to monitor Y2K issues' and putting up a Web page about the problem.

"Hmm. Better stock up on candles and batteries, Texas.

"Other states? In May, Florida Power & Light reported that

two-thirds of the way through its Y2K remediation schedule, it's about halfway finished. In Pennsylvania, the $2 billion electric utility Conectiv brags that it will spend all of $5 million to fix its Y2K problems, and it has seven programmers working on its 25 million lines of code. But the seven programmers will be able to check and fix only a small fraction of those 25 million lines of code.

"More: About 20 percent of U.S. electric power comes from nuclear plants. But the Nuclear Regulatory Commission is required by law to shut down plants that cannot show they can operate safely. In June, the NRC wrote the operators of America's 108 nuclear plants, demanding a statement of compliance, or concrete plans to be compliant by the end of 1999. The number of compliant plants so far: 0.

". . . Still, it would be unfair to say that electric utilities have done nothing. Many have spent a great deal of time and money, invariably on fixing their billing systems for Y2K.

"What are we going to do? No one knows. Many power-industry experts admit privately that they think large-scale and extended power outages, beginning in January, 2000, are inevitable. And one more thing: January 1, 2000, is in the dead of winter."

Chapter 2:
Faith, Church, Family, and Fear

1. Dear Karen: Friends tell me that I'm showing an appalling lack of faith by being concerned about Y2K. Do you agree?

No, I don't. I understand what your friends are saying—a person who has faith in God believes that he or she will be cared for, no matter what happens. But, one way in which God cares for us is by giving each of us a brain and a physical body with which to care for ourselves and each other. The way I see it, being prepared for hard times includes making sure the needs of my neighbors are met as well—while I'm stockpiling food and water for my own family, I'm also delivering goods to my church's stockpile. I'm talking to neighbors who are elderly, living alone or disabled, helping them to get prepared or arrange for alternate shelter if they would be overwhelmed in a crisis. In other words, I believe faith is very, very important, but I also believe that we were meant to be involved in both our own care and in the care of our neighbors.

2. Dear Karen: My spouse thinks I'm nuts. How do I convince him (or her) that the Y2K threat is real?

Often when men and women begin to talk about Y2K issues, the sparks fly! Communication problems seem to be escalating in the wake of Y2K awareness. More often than not, one person is more adamant than the other about the possible ramifications of Y2K and the tension builds as couples try to make decisions.

For some, the response may be laughing it off—the way many

people do when they are feeling uncomfortable. I don't know about you, but sometimes when people respond by laughing it makes me really mad—especially when it's my husband! Because Y2K can be so overwhelming, it's often hard not to get upset when the people you love and want to protect the most won't listen. Unfortunately, hostility can be the other type of reaction, whether through sarcasm or a raised voice.

So what can couples do? For the people who think Y2K is a major threat, they can begin by not panicking. Often, because of the obvious time pressures inherent in Y2K, in their zeal to convince their loved ones that the risk is real, they push too hard and end up with the other persons "digging their heels in" and not wanting to discuss Y2K at all. Like exiting a movie theater during a fire, walking slowly and steadily to the exit will get you out of the building safer than rushing, pressing and pushing your way out. Providing outside, credible references as well as hearing details from outside people who agree that there is a problem will often help convince the skeptical spouse.

Here are a few things to remember about good communications, whether you're trying to communicate to your husband, sister, mother-in-law or whomever.

Don't respond in kind.

Responding in kind is like throwing gasoline on a fire—it just makes it worse. As tempting as it may be to respond to them the same way they are treating you, remember "a gentle word turns away wrath."

Don't take their behavior personally.

Sometimes, people aren't attacking you—they are attacking the ideas you present. Try not to get your feelings hurt when they reject your ideas, thoughts and opinions.

Remember, you can't change them.

I recently heard a friend say, "People don't mind changing, they mind being changed." Don't try to make them understand, but give them information to help them understand. (I know this is easier said than done!)

Try to keep your attitude positive.

Find others who understand and try to gain encouragement from each other. When talking about Y2K with people you love, sometimes our sense of panic is communicated to them, and that's all they hear. Because they love us too, they don't want us to be afraid—so they think that minimizing the situation is actually helping us!

When discussing Y2K, keep in mind that we will get through this if we work together!

Being at odds with each other won't help—but don't get discouraged. Some people take a little longer to come around than others! For a young mother, worry and concern for her children is understandable. However, sometimes worry and concern can lead to nagging and badgering—two types of communication that can often be less than effective. Sometimes it takes a conscious effort to look for those times when the other person is most receptive to talking and similarly, avoiding bringing up the subject at inopportune times, such as when the other person is in bed and trying to go to sleep at night. Often a change in environment can help couples to communicate. For example, going out to dinner and talking over a meal can often create an atmosphere that is more conducive to open discussion. Finally, it's important to realize that while some people immediately understand the ramifications of Y2K and are ready to take action and make preparations, others may find it difficult to comprehend.

In the end, it doesn't really matter who's right about the magnitude of the Y2K problem. It doesn't matter whether you think the worst thing that will happen is that your VCR's programming might get messed up, or whether you think the Y2K problem will plunge our society into a major upheaval. What matters is that you take steps to prepare now for something you can see coming. You'll give yourself a tremendous sense of relief knowing that you took steps to keep your family safe—whether from Y2K or El Niño. Then you won't have to lose sleep as the date gets closer. You can rest assured that you've done whatever you could to weather the uncertainty.

I do think it's important to approach the issue as a united front, for the sake of your children and for the fun you can have working on a project together. Explain to your spouse that you're not adopting the "kook" attitude—in other words, you're not actually HOPING for a crisis, which is a mindset I think a few extreme survivalists seem to have. Instead, explain that for the very few who say it's not a problem, there are multitudes of credible, high-profile experts who say otherwise. With this in mind, isn't it logical and rational to prepare for the worst, and hope for the best? It is no less sensible than carrying a spare tire in case of a flat, or carrying homeowner's insurance in case of a fire. And, because you're stockpiling "real food," and rotating through your pantry regularly in order to keep everything fresh, you're ensuring that your loved ones will be well-fed in ANY crisis, including such things as an unexpected layoff from work. And, once the coffers are filled, it doesn't cost you a dime, because it's food you're constantly drawing from and replenishing—nothing gathers dust, nothing goes to waste.

3. Dear Karen: The idea of living without electricity and telephone terrifies me. How can I cope with this fear? Should I keep my feelings from my family? I feel like I'm "losing it!"

I do understand. The less experience you've had living without modern conveniences and communications, the scarier the prospect. But believe me, if I can warm up to the idea, anybody can—I am about as much a technology junkie as you could find (if it weren't for my microwave oven, I think there have been times my family simply would have starved!). But when I learned that the Y2K problem was real, and that people really were at risk of being cut off, possibly for several months, from utilities, phones, banking and so forth, I started doing my homework. I learned about all kinds of ways we can prepare ourselves to live quite comfortably and safely, without all the services that are vulnerable to this computer problem. And I learned that it's just like any other kind of challenge: if you're prepared for it, it's no big deal. In fact, it can be fun. Instead of feeling overwhelmed by thoughts about how difficult it might be, focus all that energy on getting your household prepared. Instead of allowing your fear to spread to other members of your family, start having weekly family meetings. Explain what the problem is, how it can affect everybody, what will need to be done to get ready, and why. Get family members involved in solutions, rather than obsessing about problems. Let each member take responsibility for one or more specific jobs, then at each weekly meeting everybody can report their progress and talk about obstacles or problems they're having, so the whole group can pitch in with their ideas. This Y2K thing really is a great adventure, and I would encourage you to look at it in that way. It's an opportunity for you to get back in touch with day-to-day "real living," and for your family to get back in touch with each other—free of TV, telephone, and other distractions.

4. Dear Karen: I'm really scared about this problem and don't know what to do. I don't have anyone to talk to me who believes there is a problem. I have read a lot of Websites with all different views, but all seem to know that it will be bad but don't agree as to how bad. I never heard of this until a few months ago when I got my first computer. Do you think we are going to be able to survive this?

These are tough questions, and I don't purport to have all the answers, but let me give you a few things to think about that you might find helpful. It's important to know that you're not alone in your concerns and thoughts. When thinking about the ramifications of Y2K, it does become overwhelming. It is also natural to think about the ethical/moral issues that accompany the possibility of a crisis. I think this is particularly true for women.

I've been involved with Y2K for about three years now and I've been gathering information for the Y2KWomen Website and working on it full-time since about June, 1998. Since I, too, struggle to keep a balanced perspective on Y2K, I'd like to share a couple of things I have found helpful (these are in no particular order).

First, I believe we need to be aware and plan for Y2K but not worry about Y2K. Worrying about Y2K is counterproductive at best, and I know that given the opportunity, my imagination can run wild and that I have to keep my thoughts in check. God doesn't give us a spirit of fear. I believe that God gives us both common sense and the strength to control our thoughts. Here's an example of what I mean.

My oldest daughter got her driver's license this past year (for any of you who've gone through teenage driving, you'll know immediately what I'm talking about!). I've done all that I can to help her to be a good driver. She took Driver's Ed, we let her drive as much as possible while she had her learner's permit (well, actually she drove with her dad—I was a nervous wreck!), and when she got her license, I got her a mobile phone to use in case of an emergency. She's a great kid and very responsible—but still, relatively speaking, she's an inexperienced driver.

So I'll admit to you, there have been times when my imagination has gotten the best of me and I have to force myself to trust her and pray for God's protection when she pulls out of the driveway. It isn't easy.

I think the same type of thing can happen with Y2K. We need to plan and use common sense, but if we imagine the worst case scenarios, it can grip us with fear and that doesn't do anyone any good. We need to be clear headed, make sound plans, and take the action needed to protect those we love with the resources we have.

I believe we are called to take care of our families first. But the next thing I think we are called to do is to take care of our "neighbors"—and one of the ways to do that is through the church—since I know that, as much as I'd like to, I can't feed everybody who comes to my door.

One of the biggest areas of risk is with our government computers—if the government isn't able to provide welfare for people (and if people haven't provided for themselves) then in a crisis, the church needs to be ready to provide for people. So one of the things I'm trying to do is to pull together information on what churches are doing and have people working through their churches. (If your church has a plan for preparing for Y2K that's working, please send it to me, and I'll post it on the site.) If we can disseminate information (and gather supplies in the time we have left) through our churches and community groups, we can increase people's awareness. Then, the more people who are aware and plan, the fewer people who will need help. Only after they are aware can people begin to plan and take action.

The church is also the place where we need to be talking through these difficult questions now, with each other and the church leadership, and getting direction on how to meet this challenge.

One woman I know said she was going to go around her neighborhood and anonymously put Y2K information at everybody's door. Another woman said she was inviting close friends in her neighborhood over for a dessert to begin to get to know them better so they could talk about Y2K. And as the mainstream media begins to report on Y2K in the months ahead, more people will begin to listen and plan. Remember, for some people, the idea of Y2K happening at all will take more than one discussion for them to come around.

It's my heartfelt prayer that Y2K doesn't happen at all. And if it doesn't happen then the churches will have plenty of food and supplies to help people who need to get back on their feet. And if Y2K does happen, then there will be alternatives for people in need.

Chapter 3:
Financial Concerns

1. Dear Karen: If the banking system, cash machines, credit cards, and government paychecks develop computer problems, how much cash should I have on hand?

Even the federal government admits there may be a need, real or imagined, to have some extra cash at Y2K time, and there's already a plan to print more money in order to meet demand. The "official" recommendation is $500 per family, and they're asking that you set it aside ahead of time, little by little, rather than make the whole withdrawal at the last minute, so there's enough cash in circulation for everybody at "crunch" time. Small bills are recommended, in case vendors have a tough time making change.

To be honest, I think it's sort of ridiculous to plop a flat $500 recommendation in our laps and expect it to work for everybody, but maybe the whole point of making the "official" recommendation was just to plant the seed that you should have cash on hand. How much cash should depend on your individual needs and on the length of your grace period.

Why not figure it this way: How much cash do you need to run your household for one month? Apply that figure to your grace period to come up with the total amount you'll set aside for supplies and essentials. Decide on a target date (when you want the total amount to be accumulated), and divide it up so you'll contribute a set amount every week in order to meet that goal. (Note: Be sure to put that money in a safe place, where it won't be stolen or "borrowed" from, whether by intruders or family members, including yourself! If you have a safe, that's a good option. If not, consider buying one, or simply walk through your house and find a clever hiding place where you can stick a coffee can full of cash without fear it'll be taken or accidentally pitched into the trash.)

If you rely on government checks to pay your bills, consider the possibility that they won't come on time. Even if you don't rely on government checks, you may want to carve a little extra off your monthly income in order to have money to make your rent, mortgage, or car payments during your grace period, so you can avoid an ugly foreclosure situation if your paychecks don't arrive and/or you can't get to your bank accounts. Even if you're on a very limited budget, you may be surprised how much cash you can squeeze out of a paycheck simply by buying generic instead of brand names, eliminating expensive luxuries (such as cigarettes, alcohol, candy, etc.), bringing a sack lunch instead of eating out, sharing a newspaper subscription with a neighbor instead of buying (and throwing away) two papers every day, etc. A little at a time, it can grow to a sizable cash cache. And again, the sooner you start, the easier it'll be.

2. Dear Karen: I heard that we should get completely out of debt, or we may lose our homes and any big-ticket items we're paying on time. But there's no way we can get out of debt by Y2K! What should we do?

You should take a deep breath and try to relax! I'm not sure what motivates people to try to get us all panicky about this stuff, but it does more harm than good. Here's the way I see debt in relation to the Y2K situation. Yes, it's true you'd be better off if you were out of debt, for this simple reason: While computers are misbehaving, it might be more difficult for you to gain access to your debt accounts and your money (including government paychecks, automatic-deposit checks, and checking and savings accounts). This could result in lost or overdue payments against your debts. But in my humble opinion there are ways of getting around this risk, some of which are easier than others.

If I had the ability to pay off my debts without going through too many uncomfortable gyrations, I would do it. Why? First, because it would unburden me of financial worries and make me a happier person (and when you're happy and unburdened, it's easier to cope with just about anything), and second, because it'd completely remove me and my family from the risk of payment mix-ups during a crisis.

If I couldn't pay off all my debts, I'd pay off the ones I could (making sure there's no prepayment penalty, or at least enduring the penalty with my eyes open), consolidate the remaining debts into combined, low-interest loan(s) if I could do so without incurring penalties (to reduce the amount of computer-generated paperwork on me), and get a couple months ahead on my regular payments. (I'd make sure the early payments were recorded as "early," not "extra." In other words, if I've got a payment due January 3, 2000, and I want to make that payment in 1999 so I'm covered for the first month of Y2K, I'd talk to an account clerk and make sure the early payment is recorded as the regular January 3 principal-and-interest payment, rather than just an extra payment against the principal, which would make it look like I missed the January payment.)

If I had an overwhelming level of debt and an inkling that I might have to default on some or all of it, I'd get myself hooked up with a credit counselor NOW so I could find out why I was in this fix in the first place, and take steps to get the problem resolved before computer problems made it worse.

I'd make darned sure my critical, big-ticket payments (mortgage, car, whatever) due in January 2000 are made (and recorded!) ahead of time, and if I could afford it, I'd try to make all the payments that'll be due during the next three to six months (or however long you feel comfortable), before the Y2K transition. (In other words, if my grace period is six months, I'd try to get the January-through-June, 2000, payments made before January 1.) Make sure to have hard copies (printed documentation). That way, those payments for our home and other critical possessions are recorded while all the computer systems are up and running, which protects us against late penalties and foreclosure during a period of bumpy computer behavior. Then, if the best-case scenario happens and there's only a brief interruption of services at the Y2K transition, we get to coast through a glorious period free of big bills. What a great way to ring in the new millennium!

If making early payments isn't an option, I'd do my best to make sure I had a computer-free way to pay my fixed bills when they came due. That means setting aside cash ahead of time, and tucking this stash in a safe place so I've got it when the bills have to be paid. (It's never a good idea to send cash via U.S. Mail, and to my knowledge none of the courier services such as UPS and FedEx will insure a cash delivery.) If money were tight and I felt I barely had enough to live from paycheck to paycheck, I'd start now (the sooner, the better) and set aside a little at a time—I'm always amazed how much I can squeeze out of a tight budget if I do it a little at a time.

There are two books on this topic that I think may be helpful. What follows is the essence of what I learned from them as it relates to Y2K, since neither of them was written specifically from a Y2K perspective.

The first is called *Debt No More: How to Get Totally Out of Debt, Including Your Mortgage*, by Carolyn J. White. I recently met Carolyn at a conference in California. She is quite a remarkable woman! Briefly, Carolyn had built up a very successful business, then due to unforeseen circumstances, she ended up bankrupt and now has worked her way back up to financial freedom. In her book, she addresses and gives very practical advice on how to get out of debt, and gives examples of things she learned along the way. Not only does she explain the pitfalls of various types of credit cards, she also looks at reasonable ways to save money—money you can re-allocate for Y2K.

The very first thing she recommends is taking a hard look at where our money is currently going (this is pretty scary!). If you haven't done it in awhile (and I applaud those of you who have!) figure out your present financial condition. Put down on paper or a spreadsheet exactly where your money is being spent. Carolyn says, "Keep a log of everything you and your family spend your money on for a month, and then separate this into categories of food, transportation, etc. This will be quite an eye opener for you, and will enable you to make the necessary adjustments to your spending and lifestyle which will allow you to re-direct some extra money each month to help pay off existing debt." List everything: taxes, insurance payments, loans, plus all your household expenses.

If you come out on the plus side, figure out how much money you can spend on Y2K preparations and prioritize those things you think are most important to get first. If you come out on the negative side, begin to look at ways to both save money and make a little more money (Carolyn has some good common sense suggestions like having a yard sale, etc.).

Handling credit card debt is a big subject, and Carolyn covers it well and in a way that is not too complicated. I know debt can be overwhelming and sometimes you may have a "why bother" attitude, but hopefully, Carolyn's book can give you a start at getting a handle on it.

Another book is Suze Orman's *The 9 Steps to Financial Freedom: Practical and Spiritual Steps So You Can Stop Worrying*. This book is on the *New York Times* Bestsellers List, and I've seen it just about everywhere. This isn't your normal, boring financial investment book. Orman says, "Before we can get control of our finances, we must get control of our attitudes about money, feelings that were shaped by our earliest experiences with it. Letting go of these anxieties and creating new attitudes are the first step." So this book is very different in that it looks at how our past influences our financial future and does it in a very readable way. Okay, so what does this have to do with Y2K? Well, if you find the financial world confusing (or, like me, have never been interested up until now!), Orman gives clear, easily understandable descriptions of investment and financial topics.

So, for example, if you have a husband who has always handled the finances and you're now making tough decisions about liquidating your 401(k), she explains exactly what a 401(k) is and how it works (she deals with various other financial topics as well). And as I said, amazingly, she makes it pretty interesting reading!

Remember, she is not writing about Y2K. Married or not, if you are in the throes of making difficult decisions about your finances and feel like you need to know more, I think Orman has some very helpful explanations.

3. Dear Karen: Should I cash in my IRA, 401(k), Keogh, my kids' college funds, stocks and bonds, and withdraw all the money from my savings account?

I think this is one of those areas where you really have to try to remain calm and not make any rash decisions, and taking financial advice from people who really don't know what they're talking about (like me!) is exactly what you should avoid at all costs. So, I'm not going to tell you what to do with your money. Instead, ask your financial advisor. If he or she scoffs at your questions, ask for a referral to another advisor who is willing to give your concerns the respect and attention they deserve.

I'd recommend that you take a look at Tony Keyes' articles at the Westergaard Website (www.y2ktimebomb.com). Tony also has a radio show for Y2K financial concerns on his *Y2K Today* broadcast. Here is one of his articles:

Westergaard Year 2000, July 16, 1998, *Am I Going Down with My 401(k)?* By Tony Keyes

"Let's start with 401(k)s and Keogh plans, for they have different constraints from IRAs. If you have a 401(k) from a previous employer, you can roll the assets within into another qualifying account. This allows you to choose a plan and administrator that provides greater flexibility than you might have in your current account. For instance, U.S. government gold and silver eagles qualify as investments in tax-deferred plans.

"If, however, you have an active Keogh plan or are still employed by the company funding your 401(k), you are basically stuck. There are some things you can do, however, to limit your exposure.

"Consolidate your investments in the plan into U.S. government bonds. While there are very few choices available in many plans, U.S. government bonds are almost always available. You want to move out of growth, small cap and/or income funds. These are highly vulnerable to a negative, Y2K reaction in the stock market. Remember, I said U.S. government bonds. You want to stay away from municipal bonds. In many cases, municipalities will face enormous Y2K problems and subsequent costs. Moreover, the very income-generating projects the bonds funded may be crippled by Y2K and, therefore, may stop generating income. We could see many municipalities face insolvency.

"This first approach doesn't protect you from institutional failure by your plan administrator or the federal government, but your options are very limited. If you don't expect to need your funds for the next 3-5 years or more, you may not have a problem. We will recover at some point, and you might make out all right. There is, however, another strategy:

"Many plans offer the ability to borrow against your 401(k). In this event, you could borrow the maximum amount possible and place [some of] the funds in a safe deposit box. You might not have access to it for a few days, if the vault doesn't open, but you won't be exposed to bank runs. Once the dust settles, you can redeposit the funds, however, if you need it, you have cash available to you.

"Lastly, you need to keep excellent records. One nice thing about 401(k)s is that the deposit and withdrawal activity is regular and consistent. Once you have established an investment pattern, your account is less likely to have major fluctuations like a checking account might have.

"It is very important that you consult your personal financial advisor before making any of these moves. Everyone's individual situation is different. You should design a strategy that is right for you. The rules governing these plans can be confusing for the average citizen, and it is always best to have professional advice."

4. Dear Karen: If my bank's computers shut down, how can I make sure my accounts don't get lost in the shuffle? Should I withdraw my money and stick it under the proverbial mattress?

You need to ensure that your account is preserved by written proof that it exists. That means you should always keep a copy of your latest bank statement, which includes the account number and the most recent balance. Keep this and other important account papers (such as insurance policies, certificates of deposit, treasury bills, mortgage balances, and so forth) in a central location, where you'll know where they are and can grab them when you need them. You do want to have cash on hand but the mattress is probably the least secure place in your home! Yet, if you hide money, always make sure that you can remember where you put it!

Chapter 4:
Food Storage

For a "Check List" of the things you need for your home, please see the back of the book!

1. Dear Karen: How do I make sure the food I store will not spoil?

All canned goods are required to be marked with a date or code—the problem is, most of those codes are virtually impossible to read! I spoke with James Stevens, author of *Making the Best of Basics*, and he said that even the store managers can't read the codes. So what do you do? Well, if you can easily figure it out, buy the latest date you can find. But then don't worry. Most can goods will last around two years. And even after that time, some foods will be okay, even though the nutritional content may not be 100%. Obviously, common sense comes into play here. Don't buy dented cans. *If a can bulges or you see rust, throw it out!* But otherwise, they'll keep for a long time (I know I have found things in the back of my pantry that have been there forever and they have been okay!). If you can, mark what you buy with an indelible marker with the date you got it. So for the most part, you can relax. I know I don't have the time to call and research every can I buy—again, just use common sense.

One question I had for James was about tomato products since there are so many things that we love that involve tomatoes and he said that you could find boxes of Italian tomatoes now that are really good and you don't have the acidity problem that happens with cans! (He said he found them at Sam's.) I thought this was great news!

I also found this great little booklet called *Can Opener Cooking* by David and Anita Smither (you can order it by sending a check or money order for $5.00 to Trinity House Publishing, P.O. Box 6582, Lubbock, TX 79493). They wrote it for their college age son so he could use just a manual can opener, a variety of canned goods and a little camp stove and be able to survive! It is a gem for Y2K preparations!

Still, if you're buying packaged goods, check the label for expiration dates, and buy only those items that have a shelf life that's at least twice your comfortable grace period. If you're buying in bulk at a grocery store or a warehouse-type buying club (like Sam's Club, Gemco, Costco, food co-ops, and the like), there's often an expiration date on the display bins, on the original shipping package the food was in when it arrived at the store, or on the manager's clipboard in a back room somewhere—you can always ask a clerk to look it up for you. If you're buying, say, dried beans directly from the source (like from a farmer's market), the shelf life will depend on lots of variables, such as when the crop was harvested and how it was dried and stored before you bought it—you could ask six people for an opinion and get six different responses. I recommend that you contact someone who knows a lot about whole foods and farming practices in your area, such as your county extension agent, affiliated with the nearest university (look in the "county" or "state" section at the front of your local phone book). If all these efforts fail to provide you with an iron-clad expiration date, you might consider getting your storage foods in packages, at the grocery store, where an expiration date must, by law, appear on the label. Why am I being so nitpicky about this? Because food that has gone bad is not only lacking in nutrients, it also can make you really sick.

2. Dear Karen: If the expiration dates are okay, can't I store the food just about anywhere I've got the space?

Not exactly. Expiration dates mean nothing if your food is improperly stored. The temperature in your storage area should be above 32° and below 70° Fahrenheit, the cooler the better, the air inside the package or storage container should be dry (less than 15% humidity), and the ventilation should be good enough to prevent moisture condensation. It should be protected against direct sunlight, which can ruin stored food by accelerating its breakdown (this is true even of dried beans and grains, which many people think "last forever"). There should be no heat-producing machines near the stored food, such as freezers, refrigerators, and water heaters, and the food should not be near walls (or in an attic) that get hot in the afternoon sun, because this will cause the temperature in your storage area to be inconsistent and generally too warm, causing its quality to deteriorate and its shelf-life to shorten considerably. Food should not be stored directly on the floor, which is naturally cooler and can lead to condensation of moisture from the air.

The general rule is to store your food where you live!

3. Dear Karen: Where I live, it never really gets cold, even in the so-called winter months. How can I keep stored food cool?

If you live in a part of the country where the daily forecast always includes the words "hot" and "humid" year-round, you'll need to get even more creative in finding a proper storage area for your stockpiled food. The only practical way I know to escape heat for months at a time without power-driven cooling is to go underground—options include a basement, a cellar, or a hole in the ground big enough to accommodate one or more water-tight, critter-proof containers. Or, you can build an old-fashioned cooling cabinet which pioneers used generations ago to keep their milk and butter cool before there were iceboxes. If you live in an apartment that doesn't have a basement, a cellar, or a yard where you can dig a big hole without losing your lease, your next option might be to beg, borrow or barter for a corner in a basement belonging to a trusted friend, neighbor, family member, church or civic organization.

To overcome a humidity problem, place your food, in its own container, into a larger, airtight container (such as a sealable

Rubbermaid bin) into which you've placed moisture-removing desiccator packs (for smaller containers) or half-gallon size refill cartons of desiccator granules (for larger bins; punch several small holes in the cartons to let air circulate). You can find these items in hardware stores, health food stores, variety stores, and some grocery stores.

4. Dear Karen: I thought home-canned foods lasted forever! I've heard of people who still eat canned fruits, vegetables, and even meats, that were put up by Grandma, who died 15 years ago, and nobody's gotten sick!

Home-canned foods definitely do not last forever, but the implications of "old" cans may not be what you think. According to the U.S. Department of Agriculture (USDA), the most common problem with outdated canned food is that it becomes less nutritious and less palatable over time, because the color, taste, texture and quality of nutrients deteriorate. However, there also is a chance that as a can ages, the integrity of its seal can be disturbed, due to drying or decaying rubber sealing rings, and/or corrosion of metal in the can or lid. This can lead to food poisoning, including botulism, which often is deadly. But it's really important for you to understand that a can doesn't have to be outdated to have a bad seal.

So, for safety as well as optimum food quality, try to use canned foods up before they're a year old (if they're home-canned). Above all, discard any cans that show any evidence of leakage, bloating, corrosion or even a hint of spoilage when they're opened. Cans that have gotten cold enough for their contents to freeze should be pitched out, because the food expands when it freezes, again increasing the chance of a pinpoint break in the seal. For home-canned goods, always check for solid seals and a good vacuum, and discard any jars that have bloated lids, signs of spillage or leakage around the seals, or an unexpected color or smell of the contents. Home canning jars should be stored without any clamps or rings holding the lids in place, and they should never be stacked on top of each other, so any jars with improper seals will be able to pop their lids and expose themselves as unsafe. For optimum safety, follow the USDA's latest recommendations on canning method, level and time of pressurization, all of which will vary according to the type of food you're canning and the method of processing. For a copy of the latest recommendations, write or call the USDA / Utah State University Extension Service, 4900 University Blvd., Logan, Utah, 84322; telephone 435-797-2200. (Don't rely on older publications—the rules have changed as we've all gotten a little wiser.)

5. Dear Karen: The expiration dates on some of the canned goods I've purchased at the grocery store look like some sort of code. How do I decipher it?

You're right, it is a code, and although there's probably an innocent reason for using it, it annoys me that the average person can't look at a can of food and see an expiration date that is easy to understand. To make matters worse, every canning company has its own code, and often there's no information on the label that makes it easy for you to track down a company representative who can tell you how to decipher it. I tried repeatedly to get this information for you and kept running into walls, but then I learned that the USDA really doesn't see "age" of canned foods as a safety problem; rather, it's more a matter of nutrition—the older a can, the more nutrition and quality its contents have lost. So the real safety issue with canned foods is HOW they've been stored, rather than HOW LONG. If a can shows signs of abuse or neglect (dents, bloating, leaks, or rust), it's unsafe no matter its age. So, instead of keying in on expiration date codes, I do three things:

- I buy commercial canned goods only at stores that do a brisk business, so I know the cans haven't sat a long time on the shelf in the store.
- I mark all cans with the date I bought them, or the date they were home-canned, and I try to use them all up within a year of that date.
- I check every can for signs of abuse or neglect at the time of purchase and at the time of use, and I throw out the contents if I have the slightest doubts.

So in sum, the best answer to that question is to try to stick with newer cans, but according to the USDA, even cans that are really old (10 years or more), are still safe to be eaten—just not as nutritious—as long as they're not bloated, they don't spurt when you open them, and their seals are intact. Thus, if 10-year-old cans of kidney beans are all you've got, there's no reason to starve. My rule of thumb is that most canned goods are okay for around two years from the time you buy them.

6. Dear Karen: When should I start stockpiling food? Won't some of the expiration dates pass before Y2K?

I strongly believe we all should be prepared for periods of forced self-sufficiency, even when the new millennium isn't approaching, because you never know when some unforeseen incident might make it necessary (such as a bad storm, or a layoff from work)—this isn't wacko doom and gloom stuff, it's a simple matter of being responsible and practical. There are churches that always have encouraged their members to stockpile a two-year supply of food and water, just in case. I recommend you start stockpiling food now. It'll never go out-of-date if you follow this simple set of rules:

Instead of thinking of your stockpiles as something you'll only use if there's a crisis, think of them as part of your ever-rotating food supply. In other words, when you run out of canned chicken broth in the kitchen, bring a few cans into the kitchen from your stockpile, and the next time you go to the store, buy extra broth to replenish your stockpile. That way, nothing sits in storage long enough to get old.

With a few exceptions (I'll explain them in a moment), try to stick with foods you're already familiar with fixing and eating, that your family already loves. That way, you know for sure that nothing you have in storage is going to go to waste, and you truly can look at your stockpiled food as an asset, like a savings account, rather than a money dump.

7. Dear Karen: I've checked out some companies that sell survival food kits, like rations for a family of four for one

year, but for my family we're talking $1,000 and up! It's beginning to look like only people with money will be able to eat!

The convenience of picking up the phone, pulling out your credit card, and ordering up a year's worth of food for your family's emergency stockpile is bound to have a hefty price tag, but it's the only way some people can deal with this issue. That's fine, whatever works for them.

But I have some problems with this approach. First of all, because you didn't pick out the food yourself, there may be items in there that your family just plain won't eat. In fact, you might not have a clue how to fix some of it. This means unsatisfied palates, upset stomachs from eating stuff you're not accustomed to, and a lot of expensive but unpopular food ultimately being thrown away. It's really important to stockpile food your family enjoys. That way, you know it'll get eaten, you can use it regularly so the stockpile is constantly being rotated through, and nothing goes to waste. Remember, you're not storing food "for some emergency," which gives the impression that it's going to sit and gather dust for 15-20 years. Rather, you're maintaining a complete, well-rounded stockpile of your family's regular diet, which you're using and replacing constantly. Think of it as a well-stocked pantry. You can fill that pantry by making one hugely expensive trip to the market or you can simply buy extra food every time you go to the store, and watch your food cache grow week by week. If budgeting is a problem for you, you'll probably find the latter approach to be the best for you.

Here's an example of something I did when looking at planning for food. I went to our local Kroger grocery store and made some "Y2K" purchases.

I call it **B.R.O.S.S.P.**—Beans, Rice, Oil, Salt, Sugar and Pasta—then I add bleach to the list. How much do I recommend? Beans (pinto) 4 lb. bag, Rice 5 lb. bag, Oil 1 qt., Salt 1 lb., Sugar 5 lb., and Pasta 1 lb. Plus a gallon of bleach (non-scented). I purchased it all for under $10.

That means, if you spend just $10 per week (and you can spend less with coupons and with sales), buying these things over the course of a year (52 weeks), you'll have approximately 50 bags of beans, rice, etc. Obviously, you can vary this formula and add things that you need. But my point is that if you can't go out and make one-shot purchases of food storage little by little you can build up a supply for your own consumption, to share or to barter.

If, in a worst-case scenario, you were without power, phone, and grocery stores for longer than your easy grace period, you could meet your family's basic nutritional needs with these six food items, plus water. In other words, it's probably a good idea to have some dried beans in storage, even if you're not a bean-eater, and it's probably a good idea to have a high-quality protein source that stores well, such as soybeans, even though most folks have absolutely no idea what to do with soybeans.

As Texans, we already eat a lot of beans in our three-alarm chili and other fun dishes, so my family's okay there. But soybeans? I was at a total loss. I liked the idea of having their high-quality protein on hand, just in case, but I hated the idea of buying soybeans, only to throw them out eventually because we never used them. So, I dug around and found some recipes that used soybeans, and I mustered up my courage and gave 'em a try on my family. Some of them were unspeakably awful for our very conventional, very not-health-food-store palates, but we found a few that were actually quite delicious, and I've added them to our repertoire. (I've listed two of the recipes we liked below.) Everybody's got different taste preferences, though, so I recommend you explore cookbooks in the library or bookstore, and/or search for soybean recipes on the Internet, and do some preliminary experimenting for yourself. You'll probably discover a few dishes that are good enough to fix regularly (and nutritionally, soy products are really beyond reproach, so you'll be doing your family a great service). So, you'll improve your family's diet now, you'll be able to rotate through your stored soybean stash so your stockpile is always fresh, and you'll avoid throwing away perfectly good food.

RECIPE: *Soybean Cassoulet (Serves 4)*
(Modified for cooking without electricity) Recommended equipment: gas barbecue with two elements plus a side-burner for "stovetop" cooking, an oven thermometer, and a picnic cooler (a

cheap Styrofoam one will work fine).

Ingredients:
1-1/2 cups dried soybeans
1/2 cup dried or canned mushrooms (I like dried shitaki mushrooms, but any kind will do)
1 jar of crumbled real bacon (available in any grocery store, in small cans or jars, usually in the salad dressing and crouton section); or substitute an 8-oz. soybean sausage (recipe below)
2 Tbsp. olive oil
2 cups canned chicken broth
1 cup seasoned breadcrumbs
1/2 tsp. salt (omit this if the chicken broth has salt in it)
1/2 tsp. onion powder
1 clove garlic, pressed
1 tsp. tomato paste
Grated Parmesan cheese

Instructions:
Soak beans overnight. Drain and rinse. Put in large saucepan with enough water to cover. Bring to boil, then cover the pot, remove from heat, wrap in several thicknesses of newspaper, and stick the whole thing in a picnic cooler to keep it hot. In 3 hours, unwrap the pot, stir, add water as needed to cover the beans, and bring to a boil again. Cover, wrap up, and stick back in the cooler for another 3 hours. Stir, and test a few beans to see if they've softened. If not, add water as needed and bring again to a boil, then allow the wrapped pot to sit another 2 to 3 hours in the cooler. During the final half-hour, soak the dried mushrooms in one cup of boiling water to soften. Drain the mushrooms and sauté in 1 Tbsp. of the olive oil. Drain the soybeans. Coat a small baking dish with cooking spray or shortening. Layer half the beans, half the mushrooms, and half the bacon. Repeat with the remaining beans, mushrooms and bacon. In a saucepan, heat the 2 cups of broth. Add salt (optional), onion powder, garlic and tomato paste. Bring to a boil. Pour over the layers to cover the top layer of beans. Top with breadcrumbs tossed in remaining 1 Tbsp. olive oil. Start one side of the barbecue and preheat until the oven ther-

mometer reads 350° on the "off" side. Place the casserole on the "off" side and bake 30 minutes, adjusting the temperature as needed to maintain 350°. Top with Parmesan cheese and bake a few minutes more, until cheese melts. Serves 4.

(Note: To make this recipe in a "normal" kitchen, with lights and everything, cook the beans in a crock pot or simmer on the stovetop for 6 to 8 hours. Bake the casserole in your regular oven. If desired, substitute fresh mushrooms for the dried ones, and substitute fresh or frozen sausage for the canned, crumbled bacon.)

RECIPE: *Soybean sausages*
1-1/2 cups cooked soybeans (soaked overnight, then cooked 6 to 8 hours as described in Soybean Cassoulet, above)
1-1/2 cups cooked rice
1/2 cup crumbled bacon (you can buy crumbled, real bacon in cans or jars in any grocery store, usually by the salad dressing and croutons)
1 tsp. olive oil
1 tsp. Tabasco sauce
1 tsp. garlic powder
1 tsp. ground thyme
1 tsp. ground sage
1/2 tsp. fennel seeds, crushed

Combine all ingredients except bacon in a bowl, mashing with a fork. Add bacon. Cover and let sit in a cool area overnight. Form into patties. Fry in oil, browning all sides.

8. Dear Karen: What kinds of foods do you recommend I store?

There are lists available through the USDA/Utah State University Extension Service, which actually puts out a free pamphlet on what, why and how to stockpile food (435-797-2200), but the only list that'll really answer this question for you and your family will be a list you make yourself. Why? Because you really need to stick with the stuff you usually eat, with emphasis on items that store well, such as dried fruits and vegetables, beans, powdered milk and other drink mixes, canned fruits and vegetables, fresh foods that are well known to store well (such as root vegetables, onions, garlic, winter squashes and so forth when they're available in season), pudding, cake mixes (store bought or your own), pancake and biscuit mixes, macaroni-and-cheese mixes, canned soups, canned or dried meats and fish, canned spaghetti sauces, canned or bottled juices, canned milk, flour, salt, sugar, honey, molasses, whole grains and seeds (consider getting a manual food mill for grinding wheat and rye berries into flour, whole corn into meal, rolled oats, dried yeast, pastas, oils, cereals, rice, peanut butter, jams, condiments, and so forth.

The trick is to sit down now and write down some daily menus—breakfast, lunch, dinner, and reasonable snacks, for, say, a typical month in your household—then make a corresponding list of all the items you'd need to fill those menus. That's what you need to put in your stockpile.

Then, for super-duper emergency use, make sure there's an extra supply of my **B.R.O.S.S.P.** basics—that's **B**eans, **R**ice, **O**il, **S**ugar, **S**alt and **P**asta, enough to feed everybody in your family through another grace period. Though they're not necessarily interesting in and of themselves, a stockpile of these items (plus water, of course) will keep you and your family alive and healthy a long, long time.

If possible, learn how to use soybeans and soy products now, so you can include these items in your stockpile with reason to believe they'll be used and enjoyed (remember that I'm definitely NOT a health-food nut and that my idea of "homemade" anything is ripping open the package and following the instructions printed on the outside—so, if I can learn how to buy, prepare and even LIKE soybeans, ANYBODY can!). Soy products are terrific sources of top-quality protein, which gives you another option when you're trying to prepare balanced meals. Tofu and soy milk, both of which are made of soy, taste really good if you give them a chance, and both are available in waxed boxes that are easy to stack on shelves and keep about a year without refrigeration. The neat thing about soy products is that in addition to being a superior protein source, they really are "blank slates" as far as taste is concerned—they're basically bland, so they don't offend anybody, and by adding other ingredients and spices you can create a great pot of chili, spaghetti, stir-fry, a plate of sandwiches, or whatever, with unparalleled nutrition.

9. Dear Karen: Which is better to stockpile, powdered milk or canned milk?

If you could only have one kind of milk, I'd say canned, because it doesn't require the use of stored water. If you can afford the space, though, you might want to have both. Some kids prefer powdered milk over canned milk in their cereal (or vice versa!). It surprises a lot of people to hear that powdered milk will degrade and go stale. Usually a nice creamy-white color, milk powder starts to turn yellow as it goes stale and its protein breaks down. It tastes yucky and is an inferior source of nutrition, so keep that milk powder rotating. Rule of thumb: If you store powdered milk at 50°F or below, it'll keep about two years. At 70° F, figure no more than 1 year. At 90° F, it's toast after three months.

If you haven't done it yet, please do try some of the non-dairy milk products made from soy, rice, almonds and other sources. Because they're available in the health food section, a lot of people automatically turn their noses up at the idea, but they're really, really good. Many are delicious, in fact. And they even come in chocolate! The neat thing is, in addition to their nutritional value and genuinely good taste (it'll surprise you how good they are), they come in "juice box" packaging, which is easy to stack on shelves, and they keep over a year without refrigeration. You can even make your own soy milk by adding water to soy flour.

10. Dear Karen: Some people are stocking their shelves with military MREs (Meals-Ready-to-Eat or soldiers' rations). How come you're telling us to stock "regular" food?

Great question. Military MREs certainly will simplify your food storage needs, but there are many problems with relying on them to feed your family. First, they're notoriously not palatable. If you're hungry enough, you'll eat them, but not if there are any other choices available to you or your family. To me, this seems like a counterproductive way to feed yourself when you're under duress anyway—when the lights are out, the TV is dead, the house is cold, and there's a low vibration of anxiety in the air, you need comfort food: food you're used to, that tastes good, and that's reasonably fresh and good for you. Another problem with the MRE approach is freshness. These things can (and do) sit for years and years, because there's no way anybody's going to suddenly have a yen for an MRE. You'll use them when you absolutely must, and not before. They're not cheap and it seems generally wasteful. Finally, since the food storage method I advocate is rotating through your stockpile constantly, using and replacing items so they're never in there long enough to gather dust, you'll have fresh, real food that your family is accustomed to eating—food you know they'll eat and enjoy.

However, I have personally bought a supply of MREs for my church to hand out if there is an extreme emergency because they require no cooking. But as I said, I don't recommend them for normal family consumption.

11. Dear Karen: On your Website, you recommend that we stockpile "wheat berries." Why not just buy several bags of whole-wheat flour? What about white flour?

It wasn't too long ago that I was asking the same questions. Wheat berries, which are the whole grains harvested from the wheat plant, have a nice, long shelf-life because their outer hull isolates the wheat germ oil from the air and from other parts of the berry, which otherwise cause that oil to go rancid quickly. Kept whole, and properly stored, wheat berries can last a long, long time (even years). I heard that they even discovered wheat in the pyramids of Egypt and since it had been stored properly, it sprouted—proving that it was still good!

Once they're cracked or ground up into flour, however, it's a very short race to rancidity. (Trust me, I found this out the hard way!) Rancid flour smells "sharp" and tastes really unpleasant, ruining what would otherwise be a delicious loaf of bread, peach cobbler, blueberry muffin, or whatever. You really can't mask the rancid taste, and, furthermore, rancid food is bad for you and contains "free radicals" which are being blamed for everything from premature aging to cancer. Whole-wheat flour in the grocery store may already be rancid before you buy it—it's good for only a few weeks after grinding unless it's refrigerated. In fact, I wouldn't be surprised if rancid whole-wheat flour is the reason so many people think they don't like whole wheat! The fresh stuff is delicious—incredibly sweet. So, in answer to your question, freshly ground whole-wheat flour is the only way to do whole wheat, and whole-wheat berries are the only way to store it.

If you're going to stockpile wheat berries, then you'll also need a home grain mill, to grind the berries into flour. It's a handy thing to have anyway, because I've learned that store-bought corn meal is usually rancid, too, which gives it that bitter "bite." Get some whole corn kernels, grind them up in your home mill, and make cornbread. You'll be blown away at how sweet it is. It's like yellow cake.

Now, a word to the wise as you are shopping for your mill. First of all, and obviously, you'll want a mill that can be converted from electric to manual—this is a feature many home mills have, but you must make sure before you write the check. Secondly, if you're going to be grinding up any higher-moisture grains, such as corn, peanuts, poppy seeds, etc., you'll want the mill to have a steel burr (that's the actual grinding part) rather than, or in addition to, a stone burr. Everybody makes a big fuss about stone-ground flour, and I guess it really is better (as I understand it, it's because stone-grinding doesn't get the flour as hot as steel grinding does, which means the flour gets to keep more of its nutrients). But if you grind corn, or nuts, or poppy seeds with a stone burr, you'll ruin it—the oils will get packed into the nooks and crannies of the stone and literally pave it smooth, making it useless as a grinder. So get a mill with interchangeable burrs—a stone one for flour, and steel for everything else, or get one with a steel burr and use it for everything, or get one with only a stone burr and don't grind anything but flour in it. You can find mills at health food stores, department stores, variety stores, and through mail-order catalogs that sell kitchen gadgets and such. And if you want my personal choice in mills (I've looked into this in great detail), I can wholeheartedly recommend the Family Grain Mill, which comes as a hand-cranked model with or without an electric Bosch motor for "normal" days, for $139 to $329 depending on the features you order. To get one, call Family Grain Mill at 1-828-837-5162.

As for your question about white flour, I must reiterate that until recently I've never been a big fan of whole-wheat foods, but I know that whole wheat is infinitely better for you. So do what I say, not what I have done in the past, because old habits die hard. Introduce whole-wheat flour to your family, if you haven't already. Do it gradually, sneakily—like, substituting just a little of the white with whole wheat and slowly increasing the percentage of whole wheat. That's what I'm doing, and I'm noticing a change in my palate (I'm really learning to like it), as well as subtle improvements in the health of my skin, hair, fingernails and overall healthy functioning. Good health is always important, but it's particularly vital when we're under stress, trying to keep warm in a cold house, working hard to lug water and so forth. Learn how to use whole-wheat berries now, and incorporate whole-wheat health into your stockpile.

12. Dear Karen: I've heard cooking oil has a shelf-life of only about 6 to 8 months.

If unopened and kept in a consistently cool, dark place, oil can keep as long as a year. Olive oil is generally considered more long-lived than many other types of oils. Check the expiration date on the oil before you buy. You might consider buying several small bottles of oil, rather than a few big jugs of it. This is particularly important if you live in a climate that's warm year-round—during "normal" times you can keep the opened jug in the fridge, but if the weather is hot when the power goes out, you might end up with rancid oil in your open jug. With smaller containers, you can use it up before it goes bad.

13. Dear Karen: I'd like to dry some of my own foods from the garden. How do I do this? How should I store it after it's dried? How long will it keep?

Utah State University's County Extension Office, in cooperation with the USDA, has put out a pamphlet, free of charge, on
this very subject. You can get it by contacting Utah State
University, Logan, Utah, and asking for Extension Food Science
publication number FN-330, entitled "Home Drying of Food."
They even give instructions on how to dry meat. Before you make
plans to rely on dried foods for a real crisis, you may want to try
drying some fresh foods from the grocery store, and then taste
them and see if you and your family will eat them. For example, if
you're accustomed to the flavor and texture of fresh or frozen
broccoli, you might find the dried ones to be yucky. Better to find
out ahead of time, before you stake your family's nutritional well
being on dried foods. Here are some key points, in a nutshell (but
if you're really planning to dry your own foods, you should get,
and read, all the information you can).

If dried and stored properly, dried foods will keep for a year.
They should be sealed in moisture-proof containers and kept in a
cool, dark, dry place away from heat, light, and critters. Choose
only excellent-quality, top-condition, prime foods, which are ripe
but still firm—nothing wilted, bruised, or otherwise poor quality.

You don't have to have an electric "food dehydrator"– you can
use your regular oven or the sun just as effectively, but sun drying
is a little trickier because you don't want the food to dry too quickly (it'll get crispy, which is undesirable) or too slowly (it'll sour),
and bugs will wipe their dirty little feet on your food while it's sun-
bathing. For optimal sun drying, do it on a bright, cloudless day
with temperatures of 98° Fahrenheit or above.

Some foods must be pre-treated, by blanching, treating with
certain chemicals, dipping in solutions or syrups, etc.—how to
pre-treat your food will depend on the choice of food, and on personal taste. Specific instructions are given in the pamphlet.

In general, the procedure is to sort and select the best pieces,
wash them thoroughly, peel and/or slice according to your recipe,
treat them as required for the recipe and the type of food, and dry
them in a single layer.

Rule of thumb: it will take 2 to 4 hours to dry most fruits or
vegetables in an electric dehydrator; 8 to 12 hours by sun.

However, the drying time will vary. Fruits should be dried until they are leathery and, if they're very sweet, slightly sticky. Vegetables should be dried until they are tough or brittle. (There's a formula in the pamphlet, which you can use to calculate whether your food is adequately dried. I recommend that you get the pamphlet and do the math, to be sure your food is dry enough to be safe from spoilage due to bacteria.)

To protect against contamination by insects during sun-drying, you can pasteurize your dried product by spreading it no thicker than one inch deep on cookie sheets and sticking it in a 175° F oven for 10 minutes (vegetables) or 15 minutes (fruits). This reduces the nutrient level of the food and may scorch it, but it makes it safer.

Once your food is properly dried, it is safe from bacterial spoilage, but it has to be vacuum-packed to protect it from mold. You can get a vacuum sealer for food in a kitchen-gadget store or catalog (I got mine at Sam's). Dried products will keep for one year.

Some foods that dry nicely include apples, apricots, sliced artichoke hearts, asparagus, bananas, beans, beets, berries, broccoli, Brussels sprouts, cabbage, carrots, cauliflower, celery, cherries, coconut, corn, cranberries, eggplant, figs, grapes, greens, horseradish, edible mushrooms, nectarines, okra, onions, peas, peaches, pears, peppers, persimmons, pineapple, plums, potatoes, pumpkin, rhubarb, squashes and tomatoes.

14. Dear Karen: How do I keep little bugs, worms, and other disgusting critters from showing up in my stockpiled grains, cereals, fruits, vegetables, and so forth?

This question was by far the most often asked! Not only is it important to keep bugs and rodents from getting into your stored foods, but lots of foodstuffs (flour, rice, beans, nuts, grains, etc.) come with bugs already in them from the farmers' fields. Fortunately, lots of people had excellent suggestions for getting rid of existing critters, and keeping them at bay. These all work great, so you have several options.

To get rid of existing bugs in grains, etc.: If you have access to a deep freezer that gets down to 0° Fahrenheit (this describes most chest-type or upright freezers, not the freezer part of a refrigerator-freezer), you can kill any existing bugs by freezing the food for 72 hours. Because some types of critter "eggs" are resistant to cold and actually wait for it before they hatch into larvae, some experts recommend re-freezing the food in 2 weeks, to kill any larvae that may have hatched after your first freeze. If you want to remove the "bodies" after freezing, you'll have to toss the beans or grains in a sieve with holes big enough to let the bugs through, or dump the food onto a clean surface and pick out any little corpses (oh, yuck!), then scoop the remainder into brand-new, sealable plastic bags (such as Ziploc), and store the bags in a tight-lidded, critter-proof container such as a metal canister or heavy plastic garbage can (like Rubbermaid).

Another way to kill existing bugs is to put the food into an air-tight container such as a sealable plastic bag, then dump in some oxygen-absorber capsules (how many capsules you need depends on the volume of food being treated), and seal it up. As their name suggests, the capsules take all the oxygen out of the bag, suffocating any critters (including eggs). You can either leave the absorbers in the bag and take them out when you plan to use the food, or take them out ahead of time and re-seal the bags. Store the bags in a tight-lidded, critter-proof container such as a metal canister or heavy plastic garbage can (like Rubbermaid). I found oxygen-absorber packs called Fresh Pax, by Multisorb Industries, available by calling 888-SORBENT.

Always in search of a grassroots, inexpensive and easy way to do everything, I was thrilled to learn from several subscribers that bay leaves make a great bug killer and repellent. Bay leaves, available in the spice section of your grocery store, can be bought by the pound in warehouse-type stores and buying clubs (like Sam's Club, Gemco and Costco). For a five-pound bag of sugar or flour, three leaves should do the trick: one on the bottom, one in the middle, and one on the top (obviously you'll have to transfer the flour into a new container to get the leaves in). Store the product, leaves and all, in tight-lidded, critter-proof containers such as a metal canister or heavy plastic garbage can (like Rubbermaid). For food-grade, five-gallon buckets, put a small handful of leaves (about five to ten) on the bottom, another small handful in the middle, and another on top. Seal the top, and you're done. (I also sprinkle them generously throughout the pantry.) James Stevens, author of *Making the Best of Basics* says that if you are at the stage where you actually see bugs, the bay leaves will only keep them from moving around—you need to treat the origin of the problem.

Dry ice, which is basically frozen nitrogen gas, can be used with similar effect as an oxygen absorber. As the block of ice "melts," emitting its foggy gas into a food container, it basically crowds out the oxygen in the container and thereby suffocates any weevils or bugs that might be hiding there. The stuff can be somewhat treacherous to handle, because it's super-cool and can actually "burn" your skin, so I recommend you consult a dry ice expert for advice on how to do this. You'll also have to find a source for buying dry ice which may, in many parts of the country, be tough to locate (although I've noticed my local grocery store now has a freezer of the stuff by the door, for $1 per pound). For my tastes, there are easier ways to de-bug my food, so I consider dry ice to be low on my list of options. Besides that, using nitrogen renders grain sterile, which means that you won't be able to sprout it or plant it later.

The Best Method

Hard grain products, such as wheat berries, beans, and so forth, can be dusted with a natural product called diatomaceous earth (also known as DE). DE is a fine powder made of ground-up shells from a specific kind of sea life, and if you look at it under the microscope, you'll see that each tiny piece has sharp little edges. How does DE kill bugs? Well, if a bug tries to eat a piece of grain that's been dusted with DE, the DE attaches to its little body, punctures it and kills it. To treat a five-gallon bucket of grain, dump about a cup of DE and mix it into the grain by rolling the bucket around. It's safe for humans to eat, but if you want to remove most of it, you can do so by pouring the grain from one bucket into another in front of a fan (or stiff breeze). If you want to remove the tiny particles stuck to the grain, you'll have to rinse it in water, then pour it onto a clean towel, in a single layer, to air dry. If you can't find a source for DE locally, you can order it from Perma Guard, Inc., at 505-873-3061.

Note: although DE is safely edible for humans, some experts recommend wearing a surgical mask while working with the stuff, because they say inhaling the powder can irritate your respiratory tract. You can get disposable masks in the small utility section in most grocery stores (near the extension cords, WD-40 and work gloves).

IMPORTANT: Do not use DE made for use in swimming pool filters. Machined differently for an entirely different purpose, its edges are extremely sharp and could actually harm a human digestive tract.

15. Dear Karen: How do I know how much stuff to stockpile?

Start off by thinking small, so you don't get overwhelmed. Instead of thinking of "six months' worth of food and incidentals" (or however long you decide you need to feel safe and prepared), think of what you and your family usually consume in, say, a week. Start off by actually sitting down and writing out the items you consume in the meals you usually serve, including stuff like salt, pepper, mustard, and spices. Also, figure the supplies you use, such as toothpaste, dish detergent, bath soap, shampoo, and so forth. For any items that usually last longer than a single day, such as a bag of flour, a bag of sugar, and a bottle of dish detergent, one subscriber had a terrific idea: The next time you open a new package of such items, stick a label on it and write the date. When that package is used up, note how much time has passed. You can apply all this information to your grace period, pad it a little just to be safe (I pad my estimates by 10%), and that's approximately what you need to stockpile.

To keep myself from going totally nuts buying, paying for, and storing all that stuff, I do it a little at a time—every week, I buy more food than we need, and I stockpile the extra. You can make a game of it. If, for example, you usually buy one box of (whatever), buy two. Or, if you ordinarily spend $80, buy an extra $10 worth. Or fill one extra grocery bag. Whatever method works best for you. That way, you're not really spending that much time or money at any one time, and your life doesn't have to be turned upside-down in order to get your food stockpiled.

16. Dear Karen: What sort of containers should I be using to store my food?

Because most of the food you stockpile will be used up and replaced pretty regularly, much of your storage routine is going to be no more complicated than taking the item out of the grocery bag and setting it on a shelf in your storage area. For bulk items that don't come in a storable package of their own, you can get food-grade, plastic five-gallon buckets, with lids, free of charge from restaurants and grocery stores that make bakery goods on-site. Ice cream shops like Dairy Queen and Tastee Freeze are another good source for food-grade buckets, and some fast-food restaurants have big jars, with lids, that their pickles and other condiments come in. Empty four-pound coffee cans are also useful. Or, you can buy bulk food-storage containers from businesses that sell bulk food and survival supplies. You can also get food storage trunks from army-navy surplus and camping stores— they're hefty aluminum boxes with rubber gaskets for waterproofing the lid. If you start looking around, you'll find all sorts of options. I'm partial to free stuff, rather than buying containers, but whatever works for you is great.

After washing the interiors and lids thoroughly with very hot water and dish detergent, I rinse my containers thoroughly (until they're good and squeaky), turn them upside-down in the dish rack to dry, and they're ready to use. Depending on your opinion of plastic bags, you can either dump the bulk food (grains, cereals, whatever) right into the container, or apportion the food into Ziploc-style plastic bags which you'll set, not completely sealed closed, in the bucket; add your oxygen absorber pack (or whatever you're using to control bugs); then put the lid on and seal it so the bug control method can work.

17. Dear Karen: I'd like to store some fresh food items—the kinds of food that people used to store in root cellars for many months, sometimes even longer. Can you give me a list of foods that naturally store well? Also, how do I store all these foods so they'll last (I have trouble keeping even a five-pound bag of potatoes from going soft and sprouting)?

I sure can, and I've listed them in a table with some storage tips. Please bear in mind that there might be sub-types of each food that store better than others—for example, not all types of potatoes store well. If you're planning to grow your own storage foods, be sure to read up on each type before you buy the seeds, and plant only those varieties that are known for superior storage capability (most grocery store foods are the long-storage varieties).

It is vitally important that you buy only non-hybrid seeds, since hybrid seeds will not reproduce true to kind.

I'm sure there are items that could be added to this list, but this will give you a good start.

Note: unless otherwise indicated, ideal storage temperature is 33° to 45° F.

PRIVATE FOOD ITEM	SPECIAL REQUIREMENTS	SHELF LIFE
apples	Leave stems on, store in shallow boxes or baskets	4 to 6 months
beets	trim stem to 1", roots to 1/2", pack in damp sawdust or sand	4 to 6 months
cabbage	hang by roots, or wrap each in newspaper and store in boxes	2 to 4 months
carrots	trim stem to 1", pack in damp sawdust or sand	6 to 8 months
celery	"plant" upright in boxes of sand or soil	1 to 2 months
endive	leave roots on, pack in soil or sand	2 to 3 months
escarole	leave roots on, pack in soil or sand	2 to 3 months
garlic	trim tops to 1", roots to 1/2", sun-cure 1 week, braid and hang	5 to 8 months
grapefruit	store in boxes or baskets	1 to 2 months
grapes	select fall-ripening varieties, store 1-layer bunches on trays or shallow baskets, or hang in bunches	1 to 2 months
horseradish	pack in damp sawdust or sand	4 to 6 months
Jerusalem artichokes	pack in damp sawdust or sand	1 to 2 months
kale	leave roots on, pack in soil or sand	2 to 4 months
kohlrabi	pack in damp sawdust or sand	2 to 3 months
leeks	"plant" upright in boxes of sand or soil	1 to 2 months
onions	trim tops to 1", trim roots to 1/2", sun-cure 1 week, braid and hang, or store in mesh bags	4 to 6 months

PRIVATE FOOD ITEM	SPECIAL REQUIREMENTS	SHELF LIFE
oranges	store in boxes or baskets	1 to 2 months
parsnips	pack in damp sawdust or sand	4 to 6 months
pears	wrap each in newspaper, store in shallow boxes or baskets	2 to 3 months
potatoes	cure in cool (50°—60° F), dark area 1-2 weeks, store in baskets or boxes, keep away from apples	4 to 6 months
pumpkins	leave stems on, sun-cure 2 weeks, store on shelf or in boxes in slightly warmer storage area (50° to 60° F)	4 to 6 months
rutabagas	pack in damp sawdust or sand	2 to 4 months
sweet potatoes	cure in warm (80°-85° F), dark area 1-2 weeks, wrap each in newspaper, pack in baskets in slightly warmer storage area (50° to 60° F)	3 to 5 months
turnips	trim stem to 1", roots to 1/2", pack in damp sawdust or sand	2 to 4 months
winter squash	leave stems on, sun-cure 2 weeks, store on shelves or boxes in slightly warmer storage area (50° to 60° F)	4 to 6 months

When storing these foods, a certain amount of spoilage should be expected, but you can maximize your success by following some simple rules.

● Choose only top-quality foods for storage. Inspect each piece individually, and select only those which are mature but not overripe, with no bruises or other damage.

It's okay to brush off excess dirt, but don't wash them.

● Learn the storage needs of each type of food—some need their stems trimmed, some need to be "cured" for a brief period before going into storage, some need a dry environment, some need to be stored in a moist medium like dampened sawdust, and some need to be individually wrapped before going into their storage container.

● Keep your storage area scrupulously clean and free of bugs or rodents.

● Check your food regularly, and remove any foods that have developed soft spots, mold, or other signs of decay.

● If any of your storage foods freeze, bring them in and check their quality once they've thawed—they might be fine to eat. If so, use them up as soon as possible (they'll rot quickly).

18. Dear Karen: How can I keep storage foods cool if I don't have a basement?

It's a rare home that doesn't have at least one area that could provide good food storage, with some minor modifications. An unheated hallway or spare room, under stairs, an unheated garage or tool shed, an enclosed porch, an apartment balcony or fire escape, a crawl space, under a porch—depending on the climate in your neck of the woods, one or more of these storage options might work for your situation. You may need to pack the food in containers that insulate it from the outside, and of course this might not be adequate if your climate is severely cold, like below 0° F, or severely hot, like over 90° F. But with some careful planning and a little ingenuity, you can find a dark, cool corner somewhere that will be suitable.

If you live on the ground floor of a house or apartment building, you can build an old-fashioned cooling cabinet, which is what folks used to keep their milk and butter cool before they had iceboxes or refrigerators. It's a concept that still works remarkably well, but it's fallen by the wayside as our society has become technology-dependent (which is what got us in this predicament in the first place). You can find plans for building a cooling cabinet in many books, including Rodale's Home Food Systems, but the basics, in a nutshell, are as follows: It's a floor-to-ceiling cabinet. In the floor is a hole, to access the cool, night air that "lives" in the dark space beneath your dwelling, whether that space is a basement, cellar, crawl space, or just an undeveloped area of the foundation. There's also a slightly smaller hole in the ceiling, to which you'll attach a vent. The cool air from below will circulate constantly, up from under the building, through the cooling cabinet, and out through the ceiling vent. The cabinet works well, even in very warm climates, as long as the temperature cools down at night, providing the cool air for your floor hole. You'll have to put fine-mesh screening in the holes to keep out bugs, plus woven hardware cloth in the lower hole to keep out rodents, and the upper hole will need a hood and screen to keep out critters, rain and debris (such as leaves). Inside the cabinet, install several shelves, which should be made of screening or hardware cloth (so the air can pass through them), with wooden frames for strength. Make sure the bottom shelf is several inches off the ground, so it doesn't block the air hole. Although it isn't necessary, it really helps to keep the air cool inside the cabinet if you build a separate door for each shelf or pair of shelves, so you can get to a particular food item without letting out all the cool air in the entire cabinet. And, because the floor and ceiling holes can let cold outside air into your house, you might want to insulate the cabinet and make sure the doors fit very snugly so you keep your house temperature comfortable. Put the foods that require the coolest temperatures on the lower shelves and the ones that like it a little warmer on top. Don't cram so much food into the cooling cabinet that you block air flow—remember, air must be able to circulate from bottom to top in order for the cooling principles to work.

19. Dear Karen: What if we want to go ahead, "get back to basics," and be able to provide food for ourselves?

A good source for gardening information is a book called *Square Foot Gardening*, by Mel Bartholomew. It is space saving, and possible for all weather (without electricity). For the more pioneering of you out there, you might also want to check out

Backyard Livestock, by Thomas & Looby—if you have a little space, are interested in having a little meat around, and are higher on the squeamish scale than I am.

James Talmage Stevens has written *Making the Best of Basics* and its follow-up, *Don't Get Caught with Your Pantry Down*, both of which deal with family preparedness, specifically food storage and supplies. Without a doubt, they are the best books around on the subject of food storage.

Chapter 5:
Food Preparation

1. Dear Karen: I'm not at all sure I can survive without brewed coffee! Is there a way to make decent coffee without my coffee machine?

Absolutely! In fact, according to *Cooks Illustrated* magazine, the BEST home-brewed coffee is made by the "manual drip" method—you can't get any more low-tech than that. For excellent, hot coffee that stays hot for hours, buy a plastic drip cone and a good insulated Thermos of appropriate size for your coffee intake. The plastic cone sets over the Thermos (the cone alone costs about $5, and it's available in the coffee section of many grocery stores; also available in variety stores, kitchen stores, and shops that sell gourmet coffee beans). Set a #2 filter in the cone, spoon in the appropriate amount of fine-grind or drip-grind coffee, and pour the appropriate amount of boiling water over the grounds in batches until it's all in.

I also have a French press coffee pot where you put the grounds in, add hot water, wait a few minutes and then push the plunger down to press out the coffee grounds. I make my coffee this way all the time now, and it's fabulous. (Just for fun, a friend of mine used his French press coffee pot to sprout seeds. He put in the seeds and then rinsed them with water and pushed out the excess water. It worked great! I thought it was hysterical and very creative!)

2. Dear Karen: How do I cook without the usual appliances?
There are lots of user-friendly options for cooking without

electricity. For roasting meats and vegetables, a gas (propane) barbecue grill is a must-have—in fact, a lot of people use gas grills all the time, even in the dead of a cold winter when the lights are on! Set yours up outside (NEVER inside), under shelter so rain or snow doesn't fall directly on it (or on your food, when the lid's up). It doesn't take much space—even a two-foot-wide apartment balcony will do just fine. Get yourself a rugged outdoor kerosene lantern to hang nearby, so you can see the food if you're cooking after dark. I like the Dietz brand of lanterns, which most hardware stores and department stores have—these rugged little lanterns have proven themselves over the years, they're cheap ($15 to $20, depending on size), and they can be brought inside for supplemental light as well. By the way, I recommend you use CANDLE OIL, not lamp oil or kerosene, as the fuel source if you're going to bring the lantern inside—candle oil burns much more cleanly, with almost no smoke, smell or fumes. For pan cooking, you can get a gas grill that has an actual gas burner element as an extra feature—I highly recommend this. Otherwise, it'll take forever to get the water boiling for coffee.

3. Dear Karen: Okay, I can see boiling water, heating canned peas, and roasting chicken and potatoes on the grill. But what about baking? Can I actually bake bread and cake and stuff like that in a gas barbecue?

Yes, you can. Get a barbecue that has two internal elements, so you can light them both for big meals, or leave one off, and get an inexpensive oven thermometer (about $3 from variety stores). Prepare your bread dough (or whatever), preheat one side of the barbecue with the oven thermometer hanging on the OFF side, and when the temperature is right adjust the gas to keep it that way and set your baking goods on the OFF side, so it's heated indirectly instead of setting right over the flame. If you're going to bake something sweet, like a cake, you'll have to remove any wood-smoke-flavored bricks and make sure the inside of the grill is clean, or your cake will taste smoky and have a gray-black film on it. Yuk!

Another option for baking is the ***Global Sun Oven,*** an ingenious device that bakes foods by harvesting and concentrating the sun's energy. I've got one and tried it in my back yard, and it really works, achieving standard oven temperatures and cooking things as well, if not better, than your conventional oven. The only variable is the sun—if it's not a consistently sunny day, or if the sun is getting low in the sky, you may be frustrated and/or your cooking time will drag out a bit. But if you choose your baking days wisely, making pudding on cloudy days and cranking out lots of homemade bread and cake and muffins when the sun is out in all its glory, you'll absolutely love the novelty, effectiveness, and absolute freedom from fuels that you get from the Global Sun Oven (see recommendations at the end of the book).

There is also information available on building your own solar oven in a book titled *Solar Cooking: A Primer/Cookbook*, by Harriet Kofalk, available from Book Publishing Company, P.O. Box 99, 156 Drake Lane, Summertown, Tennessee. It is complete and simple in its instructions for constructing your own solar cooker with only newspaper, foil, cardboard boxes and the piece of glass for the top. It also contains recipes.

If you live in a climate with lots of intense sunshine, another idea I heard of was to use a wok (with a glass lid) for cooking. Apparently, it acts like a little oven. I thought it was a great idea!

One of the best options is the ***Volcano Cook Stove*** (see recommendations at the back of the book). It uses a small number of easily available charcoal briquettes. This is a super "grill" that we use outside anyway because it is great for cooking. It has the added benefit that it really can be a stove used for camping (ugh) or just baking bread (for whenever my husband wants to bake bread!). It also is safe to use with kids around because the outside and bottom don't get hot.

4. Dear Karen: How am I supposed to make bread in a cold house? There's no way it's going to rise!

If you know anything about me, you know my idea of home-baked bread is plopping the mix, the water and the yeast into my electric bread machine and hitting the "on" button. But in writing this book I've done some homework, and I've learned some things that will help you. The trick to getting bread to rise is two-fold: First, make sure your yeast is alive and well, by dissolving it in nice warm water that's not too hot (which will kill it) and not too cold (which will fail to activate it). To tip the scales in your favor, use Rapid-Rise yeast, which can actually be dumped in with the flour, without first dissolving it and waiting for it to show signs of life (but beware—Rapid Rise is just as susceptible to being killed if you add water that's too hot). The other trick is to knead it until you're really tired, then knead it some more. At least 10 minutes of vigorous kneading, preferably 20. The more you knead your bread, the longer you'll stretch the elastic strands of gluten inside the dough, and the better it'll rise. As an added benefit, the kneading process warms the dough (and you!) which also helps it to rise. If the house is really cold, consider using a power inverter to which you can plug in a heating pad (the kind you use on a stiff neck). Put the dough into the loaf pan, cover it loosely with plastic so it doesn't dry out, set the pan on top of the heating pad, and invert a corrugated cardboard box over it. Use a box that's big enough to cover the pan, but not so big that the heat will get lost in there. Throw a couple of towels, a quilt, or a space blanket over the box to help hold in the heat, and your bread will rise like gangbusters. If you don't have any way to power a heating pad, and you don't have a fireplace or wood stove to set your rising dough beside, put the just-kneaded, warm dough inside a thick cardboard box, big enough to accommodate the fully risen loaf but small enough to hold in the heat that's already in the dough. Cover the box with towels, quilts, space blanket, winter coat, or whatever, and let it rise by virtue of its own heat. If you think supplemental heat is needed, you can boil some water over your barbecue pan element, pour it into a jar or bottle with a lid, and set it inside the box, alongside the loaf pan. To bake the bread, follow the instructions described in question three, above in this chapter.

Chapter 6:
Women's Concerns

1. Dear Karen: This is a really difficult question for me to ask, but should I postpone getting pregnant until after Y2K?

I was amazed by how many people have asked me this question. Many women have told me tales of heartbreak due to previous miscarriages and stillbirths, and for those folks I think it's wise to hold off if you can until after January of 2000. A history of difficult pregnancy or problems with previous births certainly doesn't guarantee there'll be problems with the next one, but why knowingly put yourself in a situation where medical care might not be readily available and the phones might not be working to call your favorite doctor or midwife? Emotionally, you're probably already pretty fragile about this issue, and you should protect yourself against getting hurt again.

For those of you who will be pregnant and near-term at Y2K no matter what anybody says, please relax and be happy. Birthing is not technically a medical condition, despite what we've all been taught since day one—a woman's body was designed to reproduce, and as long as you're generally healthy and take good care of yourself, you can trust your body to know what to do. It should come as no surprise, however, that I recommend advance planning for the big day! Learn as much as you can about home birthing, if it comes to that, either through choice or because you can't get to a hospital. There are lots of excellent books on the subject, midwives in your area, and millions of women across the globe who have done it and would probably love to counsel you and your husband. Start to educate yourself now, so you're well prepared when the time comes. I recommend you start in the library, and while you're there, check your local yellow pages directory for listings of midwives (if there's no listing, ask your physician for a referral).

Do what you can to ensure you'll be surrounded with reliable helpers on the big day, by making sure everybody in the family (or neighborhood) is up-to-speed on what to expect and what they might be asked to do. Stock up on whatever supplies you may need, plan a "birthing area" that can be kept warm and well-lit if the power goes out and remember that this is a natural, beautiful process that's gone on for centuries without high-tech intervention.

To be complete, though, you should have a contingency plan in case there's trouble of any kind—a cell phone (which might or might not work in Y2K, depending on whether the signal must go through ground stations that are either noncompliant or without electricity), a CB or ham radio, a family member designated to be the official "runner" if these communications systems fail, a snowmobile, a bicycle, a gassed-up and reliable car, an alerted neighbor—as many of these and other options that suit your situation. Nine out of ten births occur without a single hitch, but in my opinion it would be tragic if you or your baby were harmed simply because of lack of advanced planning.

There are other things to consider besides the actual birth.
- Do you plan to breastfeed? Make sure you have someone experienced who can help you should you have problems breastfeeding. Although I strongly advocate breastfeeding, I know from experience it can take some work, even if you have the best of intentions, and support is really helpful. (For emergencies, if moms are forced by unusual circumstances to not breastfeed, you may want to have some formula available.) If you plan to breastfeed, in case you develop mastitis (a breast infection) or have any problems with lactation, support is absolutely essential.
- Do you have a way to keep yourself and the baby warm and dry, even if the power is out?
- Do you plan to use disposable diapers, or cloth ones that will require washing? Don't choose disposable for "laundry

reasons" until you check out the mechanical washing machine. You might also want to check out diaper liners, which come in a roll of 100 liners for about $7. Each sheet sticks to the cloth to keep "poop" off your cloth diaper. Just peel used sheet off diaper and dispose. Laundry is less "icky" and much more amenable to hand-washing and getting the diaper really clean.

These are just some of the factors you'll have to consider as you're making your plans. If you live in northern Minnesota and don't have a wood stove or a vehicle with 4-wheel drive, a forced home-birth in January, without heat or electricity, while the wind howls and the windows rattle, sounds like a nightmare to me, but I'm a dyed-in-the-wool city girl, in complete awe of women who have a more pioneering spirit. Whatever works for you is wonderful—as long as it's a decision you make with your eyes open and your path planned.

2. Dear Karen: This may sound too silly, but since you write from a women's perspective, what about handling my period without electricity or running water?

Feminine protection is a sensitive area but one that needs to be addressed. As you may know, I have two teenage girls, so feminine protection is of great concern at my house! I'll admit, up front, to being a "nineties" woman. The idea of riding in a covered wagon in pioneer days as our "foremothers" did—without modern sanitary supplies—is beyond my comprehension! So from the start, when I heard about possible disruptions in consumer goods, what to do about tampons and pads was one of the first questions that came to mind. Along with my food storage list, sanitary supplies were right up at the top. I started buying extra. But after just buying and storing extra, there are two products I discovered.

The first is a non-disposable "menstrual cup" called *The Keeper*. This is a reusable device that will last for around ten years. It's sort of like a reverse tampon—instead of absorbing the fluid, it collects it, and you simply empty it. Now before you get totally grossed out, let me explain a couple of things.

First, after researching this product and ordering three for myself and my girls, I realized that the idea of a menstrual cup was what was so foreign to me. You see, I've been totally raised on disposable products and the advertising that sells them. I didn't know there was any alternative. And selling disposable products is big business. Frankly, when I first heard about this product, I didn't want to think about it either. But then I thought about what would happen if we didn't have access to disposable products . . . and I began to think differently.

I knew having something was better than having nothing (particularly in this area!). In fact, after researching this product, its benefits made sense for use now; it is safe—FDA-approved), cheaper in the long run, and is great to have in an emergency. I admit that it takes a little getting used to—but if you are open to the idea, it is certainly worth the peace of mind. I'm ordering extras just for convenience sake (I travel a lot and want to keep one in my make-up bag). I thought this was so important that I've worked out an arrangement so you can get a discount on The Keeper and it comes with a 100% satisfaction guarantee. It's $35.00 and you can order by calling toll free 1-888-882-1818 ext. 30. (See the info in the recommendations at the end of this book.)

However, I know there are women who, for a variety of reasons, cannot use products that are worn internally. As an alternative to disposable pads, there are washable cotton (soft flannel) pads that can simply be washed out in cold water and come in various colors, patterns or just plain. These can be customized to act as mini pads or maxi pads, depending on your needs. They, too, have a storage case. Again, although these would not be first choice at my house, I'm ordering these to have around . . . just in case. (You can also order these at 1-888-882-1818 ext. 30.)

I also recommend that moms with daughters who will be reaching puberty somewhere around the summer of '99 also buy products now. Puberty seems to be occurring earlier and earlier, and it is important to plan for their needs ahead of time as well!

Chapter 7:
Security

1. Dear Karen: How do I protect myself from neighbors who didn't stockpile food and water, but they're aware that I did? Aren't I vulnerable to looters?

This is only my opinion, but you asked for it, so here goes. There is strength in numbers, and there is joy in community. I believe the only way to live safely in a society under any circumstances, good or bad, is to encourage community spirit, the "we're-in-this-together" attitude. If you're a member of a church, organize like-minded members to band with you and start a stockpile of food and water at the church, to serve members of the congregation as well as others in the community. Elect one or more members to spread the word to other churches, mosques, synagogues and temples so they're actively doing the same. Or, find somebody else who'd be willing to speak to your group, and take up a collection to pay his or her expenses for travel and the like. Other community organizations, such as YMCA, Salvation Army, local hospital auxiliaries, food banks, chambers of commerce, and so forth can also be encouraged to get in on it—the more, the merrier. That way, there will be plenty for everybody, and if people come to your door in need of help, you have someplace to send them to.

2. Dear Karen: If the phones are out, and I've got no electricity or running water, what do I do if there's a fire?

Good question, and once again it's a matter of prevention and preparation. First of all, make sure you've got battery powered smoke detectors installed. Check them monthly to make sure they're working. Avoid using open flame for light—instead, use enclosed lanterns or battery-powered lights, and set any fuel-driven lights in a location where they're well away from flammable surfaces and fabrics, and where they're least likely to be knocked over—the risk of an accidental tipover is even higher in households with children, dogs, cats, or any individuals who may have impaired judgment. Never leave any sort of fuel-driven light unattended. **Have at least one fire extinguisher in plain view in the kitchen, in each room with a fireplace and/or space heater, in each room with fuel-driven light, and by the doorway leading to your outdoor gas barbecue area.** Make sure everybody in the family knows where they are and how to use them. Have a fire escape plan, including two exits, in the event a fire occurs. If there are children in the home, have fire drills so everybody is clear on what to do and where to go. Keep your house as clutter-free as you can, and double your efforts in this regard during any crisis that requires the family to live in one or two rooms of the house (a situation which naturally lends itself to clutter, crowding, confusion, and accidents).

3. Dear Karen: What about having guns?

(If you've already made up your mind on the gun issue, feel free to skip this section!)

I don't want you to "throw the baby out with the bath water"! No matter what you believe about guns, my intent is not to make you mad, but to give you information that will help you protect yourself and your family.

Now, given this, I realize that discussing guns can be very volatile. Most people are on one side or the other. More to the point, in a crisis they will either be behind a gun or in front of a gun! But I'll be up front about how I feel. I have a lot of questions and concerns that I'm still trying to work through.

I can see both sides of the gun issue. When I was young, there was an incident where someone I knew from school got seriously hurt with a gun that was unsecured and misused by kids who were left unsupervised. This was very distressing to me so I fully understand the risk of having guns in the home.

At the same time, I also believe in Second Amendment rights. We were given, in the Constitution, the right to bear arms. We should be able to defend ourselves.

Yet, because the Y2K situation is so unusual, I think it requires looking at self-defense (and guns in particular) a little differently and more personally.

One of the things that is unique to the Y2K situation is that if the police are unable to respond because 911 isn't working, they don't have transportation or whatever, it's reasonable to assume everybody is going to be in the same boat: Everybody will be vulnerable. Here's the thing that is of concern. If you've ever watched the evening news, you know that when there is widespread chaos, otherwise "normal" people do unspeakable things—things they would never do under ordinary circumstances.

I have two daughters, and the statistics (not to mention the daily newspaper!) show that violence is getting worse. About a year ago, my husband started traveling frequently, and I began to realize how vulnerable we were. I realized that in a case of extreme danger, there wasn't much I could do to protect my girls and myself. So I did something way out of my comfort zone. I (along with two girlfriends I talked into going with me!) took a course offered by the state of Texas so I could qualify to carry a concealed weapon.

I learned about guns, the laws, under what circumstances one can use a gun and then I actually shot a gun! The very first time I shot the gun I think I pointed it at the target, shut my eyes, squeezed the trigger and screamed! Fortunately, we were in a safe training area and when I got finished, I had actually scored in the top 5%!

But what left the greatest impression on me was that the instructor not only taught us about guns, but impressed upon us the importance of thinking clearly (or as clear as possible) in a dangerous situation. He made it clear to us that "bad guys" prey upon people, particularly women, who appear most vulnerable. The bottom line was that when you're not completely defenseless, you're better able to think clearly and then defend yourself and your family. I felt the course was valuable, and I began to look at things a little differently.

You might think I ran right out and bought a gun. But that's not how I work! I still needed to think through a lot of issues before I could make the decision to have a gun in my home.

A few weeks later, one of my daughters and I went to a friend's wedding in Tennessee. After the wedding was over, we went over to the bride's home in the Tennessee hills. It was a gorgeous spring evening, and we were having a wonderful time. Later that evening, my friends invited my daughter to spend the night, so I drove back to the place where I was staying—alone.

It was about an hour's drive back into town through the rolling Tennessee hillside. There were two things I noticed that night: 1) it is really dark in the Tennessee hills and 2) there was hardly any traffic on the road besides me.

I have to honestly say that I felt very alone, very vulnerable and totally defenseless. I realized that if the car broke down, I would be at the mercy of anyone passing by. Worse, I realized that if the car broke down and I had my daughter with me, she would be equally as vulnerable to being raped, mugged or other unthinkable things. That thought was incredibly disturbing to me.

Needless to say, I got back okay. But that feeling left me with quite a memory. I know that "ignorance can be bliss" but after being informed about the statistics and mindset of the bad guys out there today, I realized I need to be more careful, and I also need to think before I do things that may put me or my girls at risk.

So if there are severe problems in your community, depending on how you feel about them, guns can be an excellent choice. They don't require upper body strength or special fighting agility, and you can learn to safely operate one in a relatively short period of time. Many women find that they have a real aptitude for target shooting. One woman I know, a national silhouette shooting champion, regularly beats the pants off of every man on the shooting range. It's one activity where men and women are truly equal.

Whether or not you decide you should have a gun in your home is a very personal decision, and you should think carefully about it. When the riots erupted in Los Angeles, a lot of people suddenly decided to buy a gun for self-protection. They were unable to immediately do so because of California's waiting period. Gang members didn't have to wait. I'm sure many of them never thought through the moral, ethical and legal responsibilities that go along with gun ownership. I'm sure many of them never got a proper education on gun safety. They probably figured that having a gun was like having an instamatic camera—you just need to know how to load it, point and shoot. Well, that's not all there is to it. If you have children in your home, you need to know how to safely store the gun, and the children need to be educated on gun safety. Many gun-owner parents have successfully kept a gun in the house by adhering to proper safety protocols and education.

Basically, gun safety around children boils down to this: you are responsible to keep the guns secure from little hands. This does not mean you can hide it under blankets on the top shelf of your closet, because your children (or visiting children) will eventually find it. You must either have it under your direct control or store it, in a locked container, such as a gun closet or gun safe, and never let young children have access to the key.

Another essential precaution is to teach your children (when they are old enough) the elements of gun safety, just in case they get their hands on your or someone else's gun. Given the way our culture glamorizes guns, combined with a natural curiosity, children have a strong incentive to want to handle guns, no matter how many threats and warnings you give them. You should check with your local NRA or gun store for gun safety classes for adults and children. One book I highly recommend is Massad Ayoob's *Gunproof Your Children*. Ayoob is a police officer, a world-class expert in lethal force, and the father of two children. His brief book tells you how you can teach your children to behave safely around guns, and his advice is solid.

And remember, adults have accidents with guns, too! Keeping your gun secure and in your control is essential to everyone's safety.

Even if you think you know something about guns because your father kept a rifle hanging on the wall, you still need to get training and refresh yourself on the basics of gun safety. Too many accidents happen because someone didn't have enough respect to treat the gun as what it is: a deadly weapon. Tragically, these accidents could have been avoided if only people would have used a little more common sense.

Also, you must think about whether or not you could actually take the life of another human being in self-defense. This is not something you should wait to decide until a psychopathic intruder confronts you in your bedroom! You must think about it now. Could you actually pull that trigger on a person if you had to? Look deep into your heart, talk it over with a close friend, ask your minister or religious advisor for moral guidance. Remember, a gun is not a charm that will magically keep the criminals away, and you can't bluff your way out of a dangerous situation with a gun. Criminals know when a homeowner is serious about using it. If he knows you're not serious, he will take the first chance he can to disarm you, and he'll probably kill you and everyone else in the household. A gun will only protect you if you are honestly and demonstrably prepared to use it.

Finally, you must understand the legalities of using a gun for self-defense, and these legalities vary from state to state. By law, you are allowed to use deadly force if you're in immediate and unavoidable danger of death or grave bodily harm. You're also allowed to use deadly force to protect someone else from immediate harm. But you are not allowed to use deadly force to "teach someone a lesson" or take revenge. This means, for example, that you would be legally justified in shooting the intruder who is attacking you or your child, but you would not be legally justified in shooting a fleeing intruder who decided to hightail it out of your house when he saw your .357 Magnum.

Just having a gun doesn't mean you're safe. Thinking that owning a gun is all you need to be secure can lull you into a false sense of security.

Whether or not to arm yourself or take any other kind of steps to protect your family is a personal decision you and your family must make on your own. Whatever you decide, I hope you'll get all the facts and make sure that you're fully educated before you choose, buy, store, and possibly even use a weapon of deadly force. Personally I hate guns, but I understand why people might find them necessary for protection, particularly under unusual circumstances.

For those of you who find the idea of gun ownership to be totally unacceptable, there are non-lethal alternatives that should give you some peace of mind. Pepper (capsaicin) spray, available at sporting goods stores, army-navy surplus stores, and even at some variety stores such as K-Mart and Target, can really immobilize an intruder without doing permanent harm (be sure to get the 10% capsaicin spray, not the weaker 5% formula). Plan on paying about $10 for a palm-sized can. Before you buy, find out if pepper spray is legal in your area—it is prohibited in Canada and in some U.S. cities.

Another non-lethal option for self-protection is the battery-powered taser, which immobilizes an intruder by delivering an electric shock (it temporarily incapacitates and paralyzes him). A taser costs about $40, available at many of the same places that carry pepper spray or firearms. Again, be sure to check local ordinances so you're not breaking any laws.

4. Dear Karen: With fuel, do I only need to be concerned about fire?

Great question! There are many invisible fumes that can occur from fuels and it is very important to have a carbon monoxide detector. (Carbon monoxide is what comes out of the exhaust in your car, and it can be lethal.) Also make sure you have proper ventilation when using various fuels in your home. Never use fuels without being knowledgeable of the risks!

Chapter 8:
Community

1. Dear Karen: Nobody in my community thinks the Y2K problem is real. How do I convince them?

I had the same problem initially, but I resolved it by explaining it this way: Preparing for Y2K is like buying insurance. Nobody really believes they're going to be involved in a car wreck, but they think it's perfectly sane and reasonable to have collision insurance. Nobody really believes their house is going to burn down, but they wouldn't dream of not having fire insurance. If there's even the remotest chance the Y2K problem could affect your community, doesn't it make good sense to be prepared for it by stockpiling food, water, and supplies, which you'll eventually use even if nothing goes wrong?

As an added incentive, the stockpile can be kept current and fresh by rotating through—using and replacing your stockpiled food on a continuous basis, or regularly donating items to the local food bank or meals-on-wheels organization before they expire, and replacing those items with new. Even if the stockpile isn't needed at Y2K, isn't it a good idea for individuals, civic organizations and churches to be prepared in this way, in case the community or some of its members need help because of a power outage, a job layoff, or some other reason?

When I've been on speaking engagements, I have watched, fascinated, as some people in the audience change from the beginning of my talks to the end. They start out frowning, arms folded stiffly across their chests, believing I'm some sort of well-meaning alarmist. By the time I've explained the "insurance" concept and

pointed out that taking care of the community is what civic organizations and churches are supposed to be all about, they're nod-
ding their heads and murmuring, excited about getting started.
The biggest hurdle in getting people involved is reassuring them
that preparedness is not prophecy—in other words, they don't
have to believe the world is ending in order to set aside a few items
to keep warm, safe, and well fed if things get tough. This is rational, practical behavior, not kookiness. Carrying a spare tire in the
trunk of their car doesn't mean they believe they're going to experience a blowout, but it sure seems foolhardy to drive without one!

Many people I've talked to have asked me, "Aren't you afraid
of starting a panic by telling people all this now and causing undue
concern when there's plenty of time left?" My answer is,
"Absolutely not!" The reason I say this is that I think the bigger
issue is not panic but apathy! Panic will happen when people
haven't taken any action and the crisis is at hand.

That's why I'm trying to be Paul Revere [maybe Paulette!] to
women to help them understand why it is so important for them
to be making preparations now. For example, if I knew that flood
waters were coming to threaten my home and my neighborhood,
I wouldn't think twice about grabbing my girls and knocking on as
many doors as I could to warn people that there was imminent
danger!

Part of the problem with letting people know about Y2K problems is that it doesn't feel imminent. However, I think that's an
illusion. Here's why. You may be starting to hear about the "99"
problem. What that means is that many computer programs were
written where the numerals 99 act as instructions to tell the computer program to do something, like stop running, end or shut
down. What that means is we could start seeing problems starting
in '99 (oops—I meant 1999!).

I've digressed, so to get back to your question about what to do
about the neighbors, instead of trying to convert your whole
neighborhood all at once, you might want to choose one family
that you think might be most likely to be open to talking about
Y2K. Then if they get on board, you can each talk to one more
family and so forth. The principle being that if there are two or
three families that are all making plans, a) they can support each

other and b) there seems to be strength in numbers—neighbors may be more likely to listen if there is a group of you planning rather than you being the only "crazy" family in the neighborhood who is making weird preparations.

The other thing I believe is yes, Y2K will bring out the worst in some people. But it will also bring out the best, too. Get to know your neighbors now and become friends. At the risk of sounding Pollyanna-ish, these may be the very people whom you will be able to depend on in a crisis. It does take time and energy to build relationships, but working together with friends looks a whole lot better to me than fighting off strangers!

2. Dear Karen: Could you give us some one liners for opening this conversation with others? Most people I talk to are unaware of the problem or think "it can't really happen."

It still comes as a surprise to me that people are unaware of the year 2000 problem, since I'm involved with Y2K preparations and thinking about Y2K always seems to be in the back of my mind. When I'm talking with someone and I'm trying to find out how they feel about Y2K, I first ask if they've heard about the "computer date" problem. Either way, I briefly explain the problem and how difficulties can occur not from just the computers themselves but how the effects of computers impact all sort of areas in our everyday lives. Then I sort of pause and see what happens.

If they are curious and ask straightforwardly, "Won't somebody fix it—like Bill Gates?" and I sense they are open and interested, I give more information, like on embedded chips. Then I'll keep with them, until they get to the point where they need to just think about it awhile, so I don't push them into "information overload."

If I sense that they aren't interested in being open, but they say something like one man said to me, "Hey, there's big money at stake. I don't care how big the problem is—somebody's going to fix it and it won't be a big deal," I know that I'm probably wasting my time, and that I need to back off.

The biggest thing I've learned is people have different levels of acceptance. For many people, it takes repeated conversations before they begin to be open to thinking about ramifications from Y2K. I think it's because if they acknowledge the Y2K problem, they realize they are at risk. I've also found that giving them outside resources and documentation often helps. Y2KNET has free audio-print resources called Y2KCPR (Y2K Critical Preparation Resources) that are updated bi-monthly. You can get them by calling 1-877-4-Y2KCPR. I'm featured in their materials (blush) and they've been very supportive of what I'm doing with Y2KWomen. The August print report features articles by Michael Hyatt, just to name a few. So there's a lot of information you can get to give to your friends that may help.

But be encouraged. Just recently, I was talking to a friend and she is now starting to make preparations, but I've been talking to her for over a year! I have another friend from my church who just "discovered" Y2K about a month ago. When he was asking me for resources, he said he had never heard about Y2K until a few months ago. I said, "Not true! I talked to you about it last year!" But it hadn't registered with him until he read an article in *Wired* magazine. Then I guess the light bulb went off.

I may have said this before, but it bears repeating. I heard a friend once say: "People don't mind changing, they mind *being* changed."

So try not to be discouraged. Give people as much as they can handle and then back off until you sense they are ready for more. In my experience, I've found that arguing typically doesn't get me anywhere but being ready with the answer to their question does.

One neighborhood action might be to hand out Y2K information to neighbors, maybe tacking it to each mailbox during evening walks to 1) encourage general awareness, 2) promote individuals to begin preparations, 3) take things in bite sizes so as not to stay overwhelmed and do nothing, and 4) begin neighborhood action groups to encourage cooperation and safety and to minimize chances of people freaking out at hurting each other.

Also, White House and several government agencies, including the Small Business Administration, Department of Commerce, Department of Agriculture and Social Security Administration, have pulled together a national public education campaign. You can find out more about local events by calling 1-800-U-ASK-SBA or at http://www.y2k.gov/ or http://www.sba.gov/y2k/.

3. Dear Karen: My children have asked me to explain what is going on. How will all of this affect school? Are there special preparations we should make in relation to education?

First of all, while being honest, you should present the information in terms appropriate to the age of your child. Also, be sensitive to ensuring children that you are taking steps to making your home as secure as possible; don't present the information in such a way that might be overly frightening. Allow openings for your children to ask you questions—and listen carefully to their questions so you can be appropriately reassuring. Although Y2K can be thought of as a huge disaster looming in the distance, it can also be an incredible time of learning, service and adventure! For many children, the process of preparing for Y2K can teach many new things they may never have thought about before. Serving others by helping in the community can give invaluable experience that will help them throughout their lives. And one of the greatest gifts that kids have is a sense of adventure! The new millennium can be an extraordinary opportunity, with the right attitude, to make a positive difference in the world.

In explaining Y2K to your children, unfortunately, there isn't a lot to compare it to except the weather. You might explain that the first thing that would happen with a Y2K crisis is that they will probably get an extra long Christmas vacation because they can't return to a school without electricity! Classrooms need heat and light and unless their school has an electrical generator and the fuel to keep it going for a month, school would need to be canceled. (Now extra vacation time sounds great but remember, if they lose time, which typically happens from snow days in the winter, it has to be made up in the summer!)

Another Y2K concern related to school is if there were significant problems with the school computer systems, you may not be able to get your child's records. I would suggest that all students get a hard copy (printed paper document) of their transcripts. Again, losing your grades for some students might be an answer to a prayer (!) but think about what it might mean if you couldn't get your records (or the information was wrong) and you were applying to colleges. It would seem wise to get a folder and keep a copy of all school records including PSATs, SATs and any other important test results.

If school were to actually be called off for an extended period of time, you might want to consider home schooling.

For teens, The American School, 2200 East 170th St., Lansing, Illinois, 60438-6001, has a four-year supply of books that are reasonably priced and accredited, and, as long as the mail service continues, offers a wonderful self-study program for approximately $30.00 per month.

For younger children, the School of Tomorrow out of Lewisville, Texas, offers materials for a self-study program. Their telephone number is 972-315-1776. However, it is my understanding that a lot of this information is electronic. If you don't have power, you might need back up books!

Chapter 9:
Water

1. Dear Karen: Should I stockpile water, too? If so, how much? What a hassle!

Hassle, yes. But look at it this way: the average, healthy human body can survive over a month without food, but only a few days without water. We are, after all, 65% water, and we lose water constantly through tears, sweat, urine, feces, and the vapor in our breath, to the tune of about 10 cups per day when we're not active, and as much as three times that much when we're doing strenuous things. It also takes a certain amount of extra water to allow us to digest the food we eat—more water for dry foods such as grains and breads and meats, less water for wet foods such as stews and vegetables and puddings. So, how much water do we need to store? The rule of thumb is to figure a gallon per person per day, which should cover drinking water, cooking water, brushing teeth, and face-washing. For bathing and doing laundry, add another gallon per person per day. (I'm assuming you won't all shower and do laundry every day, and unless your hands are really mucky, a communal bucket of heated water can be used to wash several pairs, several times.) That's a lot of water, and it's an important commodity, probably the most important thing you can have in your stockpile.

2. Dear Karen: How should I store water? How long will it "keep"?

You can store water in small, easy-to-handle containers such as

1/2-gallon to 2-gallon containers, or you can store it in huge, 50- to 100-gallon cisterns which are hooked up to your regular plumbing system (the water is always being circulated and replaced as long as your regular water supply is running). The advantage of the smaller containers is cost and manageability: the cost is nil, if you're recycling juice or soda containers you're keeping them out of the landfill, and the smaller jugs are easy to carry around. Water is really heavy. Just think what it is like to carry two gallons of milk into the house—you know how heavy it gets when you have to lug them very far! The disadvantage is, it's a bit of a hassle finding truly safe containers in which to store your water (the debate on plastics, which reportedly can leach small amounts of toxic chemicals into stored water, rages on).

No matter which storage method you choose, you'll have to make sure the water is purified so it's free of toxins and potentially harmful organisms. **Properly purified and stored water can be kept indefinitely.** The current recommendation for safe containers includes glass, polyethylene, polyester, or metallized polyester. I'm reluctant to recommend glass because of the obvious risk of breakage, which not only creates a mess and wastes your precious water, but also carries a real risk of injury in a cold, dark storage room while juggling with a flashlight. Personally, I like to use the two-liter soda bottles and the half-gallon plastic juice bottles (like those in which you buy apple or cranberry juice), which my family goes through by the dozens. Again, it depends on whom you ask, but most of the opinions I've gathered have indicated that the milky, nubbly type of plastic (such as the one-gallon milk jugs) are not good because the plastic, designed to break down faster in landfills, deteriorates too quickly. Smooth, shiny, clear plastic, such as in soda bottles and fruit juice bottles is better.

Whatever you use, it should be thoroughly cleaned in sudsy water, rinsed well, and air-dried before filling to within an inch of the top with purified water (your choice of filtered, distilled, or chemically treated) and securely capped (don't forget to wash, rinse, and thoroughly clean the caps as well).

Adding three to four drops of non-scented chlorine bleach per two-liter bottle is a very cheap way to make sure you have water on hand. (I recommend this even for water you are storing for washing and the like.)

3. Dear Karen: I tried drinking some water I'd stored for several months, and it tasted "flat." Any suggestions?

After storage, water usually tastes "flat." The way it was explained to me, this is due to lack of oxygen. You can remedy this by shaking the bottle or pouring the water from one container to another, re-incorporating air back into it—this should help it taste fresh again. Another solution is to add Kool-Aid or other flavorings. I bought a large container of Tang with extra vitamin C, so not only will the water taste good, but your family will get some vitamins, too.

4. Dear Karen: Why do I need to "purify" the water that comes out of my faucet, if we usually drink it "as is" all the time anyway? What if it already has chlorine in it, thanks to the water treatment folks in my city? How do I purify it myself, assuming this is something I need to do?

Even if your tap water is drinkable "as is," it's likely to contain low levels of pathogens (potential disease-causing germs) that could thrive and multiply in long-term storage conditions, causing your water to become fouled and possibly even dangerous. When officials check the public water supply in your community, they're not making sure it's absolutely free of pathogens—they're simply making sure the level of pathogens in the water is low enough so that it's not likely to make anybody sick under normal circumstances. This is equally, if not more, true of well water and spring water.

About chlorine: Water that's already chlorinated, as is the case in many large cities, is not necessarily purified with respect to pathogens. One very significant pathogen (called Cryptosporidium) isn't killed by chlorine at all—in fact, lab tests have shown that some strains of "Crypto" actually thrive in it. An outbreak of Cryptosporidiosis, with diarrhea and nausea, occurred several years ago in Milwaukee, Wisconsin, for that very reason. So, if you live in an area where the water supply is at risk of Cryptosporidium contamination (usually that means there is farming nearby), chlorine simply won't be good enough. If you were planning to rely on chlorine to purify your water, call your local public health department to find out if there have been any reports of Cryptosporidium in the past few years. And, if your water source or public storage facility is near a farm with livestock, particularly cattle, don't rely on chlorine to purify your water, because the domestic cow is a common carrier of Cryptosporidium. If your water isn't contaminated with it today, it could easily be contaminated next month. All it takes is a new, carrier cow arriving on the farm.

Another thing about pre-chlorinated water is the fact that the levels of chlorine might not be sufficient to eliminate pathogens that contaminate the water after it leaves the central reservoir. Leaky pipes along the way, and any contamination and sediment that might be present in pipes, valves and storage tanks anywhere between the reservoir and the tip of your faucet, might overwhelm its ability to kill off even the daintiest of germs.

The bottom line on water is, you have to nip those pathogens in the bud, before they take over the water you plan to put into storage. I encourage you to do some research of your own to find the method that works best for you. Following are some of the methods I have learned about in my own research. Obviously, after purifying your water, you should store it in containers that won't reverse the process by adding contaminants and toxins back into the water.

● *Boil it.* It's time consuming, a real hassle, and not totally infallible (some pathogens actually can survive boiling, but they're usually not an issue in this country). The water must boil vigorously for 20 minutes.

● *Filter it,* with a countertop or built-in faucet filter (such as the Brita water pitcher, available in grocery stores and variety stores everywhere). The Brita filters and others like them are marketed as a way to make tap water taste purer, and they even remove some chemical contaminants such as lead, but they don't claim to make contaminated water safe. This can be a problem if your water source, and/or your plumbing pipes, already contain some organisms that are too small to be trapped by the filter, such as certain bacteria and viruses. If you have any doubts, shop around for a finer filter that is warranted to remove pathogens, and/or get your tap water tested at your local public health department first—if it gets a clean bill of health, it should be okay to use a Brita-type countertop filter as your main mode of purification unless things get really bad. All water filters are meant to be replaced at regular intervals (and sooner if you use them "a lot," which isn't defined in the literature that comes with the Brita filter)—if you try to pinch pennies and keep a filter past its scheduled discard date, two things can happen: First, it could become clogged with the crud it has removed from your water, making it work very slowly, which is a pain when you're trying to put away a lot of water. Second, the crud that naturally accumulates in the filter (instead of going into your water) can become colonized with germs and actually become a source of contamination, a problem that becomes more and more of a probability the longer you keep the filter. So, be diligent about changing filters when you're making purified water for storage. And remember that if you're using water of questionable integrity to begin with, this sort of filtration may not be adequate.

● *Filter it, with a millipore filter:* These are available in desktop models or in a hand-pump-style carried by hikers for purifying water they find along the trail. Because they're able to trap even smaller germs than the countertop filters are, they're marketed as a means of purifying water that's contaminated and should be fine for your purposes here. And, like the countertop filters, they'll also remove some chemical contaminants, such as lead, pesticides, detergents, and even chlorine (which chemicals they remove depends on the size of the chemical's molecules). The desktop model I'm aware of is called Amritt Vitae, available from DSK Medical Products for about $20 (for orders call 949-588-1170). Replacement filters cost about $5. The campers' models, such as the Katadyn, are available in stores and catalogs that carry camping, hunting and hiking gear, such as L.L. Bean (800-221-4221), Mountain Gear (800-829-2009), Cabela's (800-237-4444), and Eddie Bauer (800-426-8020). Cost ranges from $35 to $200, and replacement filters range from $10 to an unbelievable $50. For me, the biggest disadvantage is that they're relatively slow—some brag about taking "as little as" 4 minutes for 1 gallon of water, which feels like a long time if you have to stand there and pump the water in (I don't know about you, but I don't have that sort of patience). But they really work well, and for a single drink, they're terrific. The filter I have is the British Berkefeld Water Filter—removes parasites and pathogens, as well as undesirable odors and flavors: $259.00. Each filter includes four silver-impregnated ceramic filter elements. Additional replacement elements are available for just $35.00 each. (See recommendations at the end of the book.)

● *Add chlorine bleach* (the laundry type, without added colors, scents, or other stuff. Pure sodium hypochlorite is what you're looking for). The USDA recommendation is 1/4 teaspoon per gallon of water (or I use about three to four drops per two-liter bottle). It's easy and quick, but not totally infallible. Chlorine does not remove toxins and chemical contaminants, and in the eyes of many it is, in and of itself, a toxic contaminant. For folks who believe added chlorine is a health risk, this method can be combined with filtration, using the filter of your choice to remove the chlorine after 30 minutes (which should give it enough time to kill most common germs).

● *Add iodine water purification pellets.* It's easy, quick, and very effective (but be warned that it tastes pretty awful). Before millipore filters were available in gadgets small enough for backpackers, iodine pellets were the standard for back-country water purification. They're available in stores and catalogs that carry camping, hunting and hiking gear, and a bottle of 50 pellets costs about $5. (It takes 1 pellet to treat a quart of water.)

Iodine won't get rid of chemical contaminants, and as you may have guessed, there are folks who quiver at the prospect of drinking water with this stuff added to it. Again, filtration after the iodine pellet has had time to work (30 minutes should do it) can help remove most of the additive, leaving the water pure as long as the filter is clean.

● *The Steri-Pen* is a neat new gadget that'll work great for a single glass. It's about the size of an electric toothbrush, and its battery will last for about 30 treatments. The business end emits ultraviolet light which, when immersed in your glass for 30 seconds, kills germs, including Giardia, E. coli, tiny viruses, and Cryptosporidia. In fact, on a larger scale, ultraviolet light is used to sterilize commercially bottled water (again, it won't get rid of chemical contaminants). The Steri-Pen will be available in early 1999 from the manufacturer (Hydro-Photon, 207-374-5800) for about $200.

● *Distill it.* This process removes just about all contaminants, including sediments, dissolved solids, heavy pesticides, herbicides, and even volatile gases. The trouble is, it's quite slow (about 6 hours per gallon with the countertop distiller I found) and expensive, compared to some of the simpler methods of purification. Still, a lot of people swear by this method, though some people complain that by removing the minerals from the water, they're leaving us at risk for mineral deficiency! I figure we get plenty of minerals in good food and a good quality vitamin-mineral supplement, and somewhere along the line you've got to stop worrying about stuff! I found a nice distiller, called the EcoWater Distiller, in the Harmony catalog (800-869-3446) for $200, plus $13 for the filters it uses, and $14 for stuff to clean the scum that comes out of your water and adheres to the interior of the machine.

● *Buy commercially bottled water.*

Chapter 10:
Health and Hygiene

1. Dear Karen: How do I prepare for medical emergencies, in case something happens when the phones and electricity go out?

Make a list of all the medical conditions, serious or otherwise, that are treated in your household over the course of a typical year. This includes major conditions (arthritis, high blood pressure, thyroid disorder, migraine headaches, etc.) as well as minor conditions (acne, menstrual cramps, athlete's foot, the flu, etc.), and make a corresponding list of all prescription and over-the-counter medications and medical supplies you might need to treat those conditions. Add accidents, such as cuts, scrapes, sprains, bruises and so forth, and stockpile enough band-aids, ace bandages, gauze squares, adhesive tape, Betadine solution and Neosporin ointment to handle several incidents in each family member, just to be on the safe side. It's also a very good idea to get a basic first-aid book which can help you determine whether any symptoms you've noticed are serious and in need of professional care, or minor and appropriately dealt with at home. I particularly like the book, *Take Care of Yourself: The Complete Guide to Medical Self-Care*, by Vickery and Friese, but if you've got a different book that gives you the sort of guidance you need, that's great.

For emergencies, there's just no substitute for a well-organized, thoughtfully stocked first-aid kit. [See the recommendation for the Hospital-in-a-Box at the end of the book.]

2. Dear Karen: How can I get my doctor to give me a pre-

scription for antibiotics, just in case someone in my family gets sick or injured?

I've asked a lot of experts about this, because a lot of people brought it up. Here's what just about every respected physician and pharmacologist told me. Each antibiotic was developed to fight a specific group of bacteria, and there is no single antibiotic that will kill all bacteria. When someone is ill or injured, an antibiotic will help that person only if the problem involves bacteria (not viruses or fungi, which are unaffected by antibiotics), and only if the particular bacteria present happen to be sensitive to the particular antibiotic given. If you give the wrong antibiotic, it will kill off some of the patient's "good" bacteria, making it easier for the "bad" bacteria to flourish. In other words, the wrong antibiotic can make you even sicker, or increase the chances that your injury will get seriously infected. To make matters worse, if your problem is the result of a fungal infection, antibiotics will kill off "good" bacteria, which were in competition with the fungus, and the result will be a "super-infection" of fungus. So, most physicians-in-the-know agree that it's really inadvisable to give out antibiotics for preventive use.

On the other hand, if you have a history of getting a certain kind of bacterial infection that your doctor has previously prescribed a specific antibiotic for, he or she might agree to prescribe that antibiotic for you to have on hand, just in case you should fall ill during a crisis. It's really up to your physician, but you shouldn't be surprised or upset if he or she refuses. The bottom line is, you need a diagnosis before you start messing with antibiotics. You might try colloidal silver, which is believed by many to have antibiotic properties. You can buy it in bottles.

3. Dear Karen: I'm frustrated with the traditional methods of medical information in light of Y2K. Where can I go to find out if there are other options or alternatives?

My intent is not to give medical advice since I'm not a physician but I'll be happy to give you some options on where you can look for alternatives if there are Y2K problems.

Y2K can put our medical delivery system at risk. There's a

manual I've come across that is full of information on medical alternatives for Y2K. It's called *Dr. X's Underground Guide to Y2K Medical Survival.* This doctor has experience in inner-city medical emergencies as well as old fashioned "country doctor" type medicine and tells you exactly what you need to know if traditional sources of medicine dry up.

This 160 page manual is normally $199 but I have arranged with the publisher for you to get it for $97 - a $102 savings off the regular published price. You'll gain vital inside knowledge of the little-known underground emergency medical techniques and infectious disease survival strategies that can literally save your life and the lives of your loved ones during the all-too-possible medical system breakdown and ensuing infectious disease crisis. To order for only $97 plus $4.50 shipping and handling, call 1-800-552-3438 code XKB or send a check to Year 2000 Project, WAVE Publications, P.O. Box 1014, Colleyville, TX 76034.

Many people are familiar with colloidal silver, the powerful all-natural antibiotic that's proven effective against over 650 infectious disease-causing microorganisms, including most viruses, bacteria and fungi. For Y2K, there is a little known and highly effective way to produce fresh, pure therapeutic-quality colloidal silver at home, in under 10 minutes, for about 70 cents per gallon rather than the $10 per ounce charged by health food stores and mail order companies - a colloidal silver generator. There is a company that distributes inexpensive, high-quality colloidal silver generators along with an in-depth manual that gives you extensive background and documentation on colloidal silver with complete instructions on the use of this safe, powerful natural antibiotic. You can also purchase a colloidal silver generator along with the comprehensive Colloidal Silver Manual for $179 plus $5 shipping and handling by calling 1-800-552-3438 code CSKB or send a check to Year 2000 Project, WAVE Publications, P.O. Box 1014, Colleyville, TX 76034.

4. Dear Karen: What personal care, non-food items do I need to stockpile?

The best way to figure out what personal supplies you and your family will need is to go into each room of your house and think of what happens in there, then make a list of the items you need to accomplish those things. I'm talking about items that will become depleted with use, not "permanent" items such as pajamas.

In the bathroom, for example, you'll list such items as toothpaste, spare toothbrushes, mouthwash, toilet paper, toilet bowl cleanser, feminine hygiene products, products for individual problems such as vaginitis or athlete's foot or acne, shampoo and cream rinse, soap, moisturizers, rubbing alcohol, witch hazel, peroxide, deodorant, shaving cream, razor blades, eye drops, nasal sprays, cold medicines, Epsom salts, Tylenol, cough medicines, and so forth.

Then move to the kitchen: Dish detergent, sponges and pot scrubbers, baking soda and vinegar for cleaning, disinfectant for sink and countertops, paper towels, matches, candles, batteries, etc.

In the master bedroom, be sure to consider intimate items. In the laundry room, you'll list detergent and spot remover.

To figure out how much to stockpile of each item on your lists, label each item with the date you opened the package, then note the date when the package is empty—this will give you a ballpark idea of how long the package lasts.

(See the back of the book for a *"Home Check List"* of things you may need.)

5. Dear Karen: How can we bathe if there's no running water, let alone HOT water?!

This is actually a fairly simple problem to take care of with minimal pre-planning. In camping stores or catalogs, and even in some of the larger variety stores, there are simple gadgets called "sun showers." They're a plastic bag, covered with a dark-colored nylon bag that has a fabric handle on one end and a spigot on the other, affixed with a rubber hose and a cute little shower head. The bags hold a gallon or two of water, depending on what you buy. Here's what you do: Heat some water in a teapot or kettle until it's just a little warmer than you like for your bath. Using a funnel so you don't spill, fill your shower bag with the hot water. Some of the heat will be absorbed by the cold fabric and by the slight delay before you get naked, but you'll still want to make sure the water has cooled enough so you don't get scalded. Hang the shower bag from your regular shower head (if it wants to slip off, take a thick rubber band from your newspaper and wrap it around the metal shower head's neck a few times—this will serve as a stopper for your sun shower's handle). Set a lantern in a safe place on your bathroom sink where it won't get knocked off or start a fire. Then climb in the shower. Open the spigot to get yourself and your soap wet, then shut it off. Soap up then rinse yourself off. You'll be amazed at how refreshing it is to shower this way, in a chilly bathroom, with hot water! And believe it or not, there's usually plenty of water not only to bathe your body, but also to shampoo and rinse your hair. For those of you with really long hair or a predisposition to take LONG showers, buy a couple of sun showers and fill them both. That way, you'll be sure to have enough hot water to rinse thoroughly.

6. Dear Karen: What do we do about using the toilet? If the electricity is off, there will be no running water.

If you live in a home that has its own septic system, your toilet will flush normally if you dump a two-gallon bucket of water into the bowl after use. If you're hooked up to a city sewer system, dumping water into the toilet may or may not work—it depends on whether your city's system has electric switches and pumps to move the effluent from homes to the treatment plant. Call the manager of the sewer system and ask whether you can flush your toilet with a bucket of water if the entire city were without power. Don't accept a "probably" or "I don't think so" answer—if he or she can't respond with authority, and back it up in writing, ask for the name and number of someone who can, and you might want to get the local newspaper involved too. A lot of people will need to know the answer.

If the answer is "no," (or you have any doubt!) you'll need to devise an independent toileting method for your family. Your choices include a composting toilet, a porta potty usually reserved for camping expeditions, or a rented chemical toilet-in-a-box (such as what you see at construction sites). It's not a good idea to "just go outside," even if you live in a rural area, because over an extended period of time the human body can produce an overwhelming amount of liquid and solid waste which can foul an area and create additional health problems.

7. Dear Karen: How on earth will we be able to keep our clothing clean without a washer and dryer?

You've got three choices: *Hand-washing, non-electric mechanical washing, and going dirty!* Most clothing items will clean up quite nicely by hand-washing in a dishpan in the bathtub, but there are some tricks to doing this efficiently and easily. First, protect your hands by using a mild detergent such as Woolite or liquid dish detergent—regular laundry detergent is far too harsh for repeated hand use, and you'll end up with a really bad case of chapped hands if you ignore this warning. Second, you'll get things cleaner if you forget about doing "a big load" and, instead, wash one or two items at a time. For really dirty spots and stubborn stains, keep a hand brush nearby for scrubbing. Make a pile of all the items you've washed, squeeze or blot out as much of the water as you can, then dump your wash water into a bucket for re-use (it'll help knock the first layers of grime off dirty hands, or serve as a "pre-wash" for really greasy pots and pans). Refill the dishpan with clear water and add a teaspoon of white vinegar for a more complete rinse. Re-rinse in fresh water with vinegar as many times as necessary to get out all traces of detergent—otherwise, skin irritation when you wear the clothes can result. If the faint smell of vinegar is objectionable, do a final rinse with plain water. Squeeze out as much excess water as you can, and hang your clean laundry to drip over the bathtub. If there's a warmer room where the family is congregating, you can move your laundry to a clothesline in that room as soon as it stops dripping.

If you find the idea of hand-washing impossible, there is a hand-cranked washing machine available for doing small loads. Shaped like a small home cement mixer, the machine holds water, detergent and clothes in a cylindrical tub with a pressurized seal, and agitates the clothes when you turn the side-crank. The manufacturer claims that the sealed lid creates a high-pressure bath that forces soapy water into fabrics, for a fast and easy load (two minutes!). You can order the hand-cranked washing machine for less than $50 through the Jade Mountain catalog, at 800-442-1972.

Chapter 11:
Care of the House

1. Dear Karen: How do I keep my pipes from freezing if there's no running water and I can't let my faucets drip?

You'll have to make sure the pipes are empty, which will require doing some homework ahead of time. In a nutshell, most household plumbing systems are built on a gentle slant, so there's a "highest" place and a "lowest" place. If you've got a basement, it should be a slam-dunk to find the lowest place, because it'll be in the basement where all the pipes are likely to be exposed anyway. If you're not sure, or you're just not inclined to understand plumbing, ask a knowledgeable friend to help you, or hire a real live plumber to come over and show you where the lowest place is. Then, as long as the plumber's standing right there, have him or her install a faucet at that location. That way, when you need to drain your pipes to prevent freezing in an unheated house, all you have to do is open that faucet and let the water drain into containers. You might as well use containers that are clean, because the water's reasonably clean. It can be run through a filter, treated with the purifier of your choice, or used for bathing and laundry. Don't forget to drain the water heater, too.

If you don't want to drain your pipes through gravity flow (for example, if you think there are places where the water can get trapped), the other alternative is to force the water out of the pipes with an air compressor. Again, this is something you'll need an expert to demonstrate if you're not mechanically inclined, and of course you'll need an air compressor that will run without regular electricity. This isn't all that complicated—air compressors can be had for very little money, as little as $10 to $40 for dinky ones or used ones at garage sales, and they can be "charged up" with air and left to sit for extended periods of time so the compressed air is ready when you need it.

Chapter 12:
Pets

1. Dear Karen: Should I be doing anything special to protect my pets?

This is an important topic, because it seems a lot of people are overlooking this "little detail." Maybe it's because our pets are so undemanding and generally easy to care for (relative to other family members), and it's easy to forget that they have important needs. As a mother, I'm very sensitive to how a community-wide crisis might affect my children, and I know in my heart that the last thing our kids need is to lose a beloved pet simply because of an oversight. No matter what kind of pet you have—dog, cat, backyard horse, caged bird, guinea pig, aquarium fish, or whatever—you need to be concerned with five things: food, water, medical care, comfort, and security. Be sure you've included your pet's needs in your stockpile of food and water, and have planned ahead in terms of medical care and any accommodations you may need to make to keep them comfortable without ready access to electricity.

2. Dear Karen: The family dog and cat live outside. Is there any problem with that during Y2K or any other crisis?

For pets that spend time out-of-doors, you should be cognizant of the increased threat to their safety during a prolonged crisis—dogs and cats that have been abandoned by their owners will be hungry and in search of food, water and shelter. This could put your own pets in the position of having to defend their territory against invasion by intruders, risking injury and exposure to diseases such as distemper, parvo, feline leukemia, feline "AIDS," and rabies, if the intruders aren't properly immunized. Stray dogs commonly band together in packs, and in some rural communities these packs periodically threaten wildlife, livestock, children, pets, and even the occasional adult human—in the event of a community food crisis, this might become a widespread problem.

To minimize your risk, make sure you keep all food locked up where "passing-through" animals can't smell it or get to it. This means that there should be no dog food or cat food sitting around (feed your outside pets at specific meal times, rather than leaving food out all the time, and pick up any leftovers within an hour). Any edible household garbage should be kept in a tightly closed bin inside the house so there are no smells to attract wild or feral animals, until it can be composted in a sealed composting container (there's a neat one available for $124 in the Harmony Catalog 800-869-3446, or you can contact your local sanitation district—often they have home composters for sale at cost), or hauled off to a public dump or landfill the next time someone makes the trek into town. And unless you have a closed container to start the composting process of wet kitchen garbage indoors, you should not include these materials in any outdoor compost pile—in urban areas they'll attract raccoons, skunks, possums, coyotes and rodents, which create problems of their own, and in rural areas you can add bears, wolverines, more coyotes and other scavengers to the list. If you're diligent about eliminating all food sources for stray animals, they'll essentially cross you off their list as they're making their rounds, only stopping by occasionally to see whether you've gotten careless. Don't contribute to the stray pet problem by allowing your own pets to roam unsupervised—if your dog or cat needs to go outside, go with them, stay with them, be prepared to protect them against predators and malicious dog packs, and then bring them back inside.

3. Dear Karen: What about households that include small animals (such as a hedgehog, a guinea pig, rabbit, etc.) or a caged bird or aquarium fish? Can these types of pets survive if we lose our heat and electricity?

For exotic animals—those that were meant to live in an environment that's totally different than the one we live in, such as parrots [tropical rain forest], aquarium fish [clean water with a constant temperature and oxygen supply], hedgehogs [forest burrows] and so forth, survival in a cold, dark house is going to require some special preparation that likely will include a supplemental supply of power and heat. Because many of these critters are super-sensitive to poisoning by toxic gases, you have to be really careful what method you use to keep them warm. Try to speak with someone in your area who is knowledgeable in the care of your particular species of pet, and has expertise in alternative methods of providing that care when public utilities are down.

4. Dear Karen: Will I need to store food and water for the family dog and cat?

It would be wise. Thanks to the availability of commercial pet food, most of our dogs and cats are accustomed to dietary monotony, which means it's pretty easy to stockpile food for them: just calculate how much of your pet's usual dry and/or canned food will be used up during your comfort/grace period and start accumulating to accommodate that timeframe. Check the expiration dates on the packages and be sure to buy only those packages that are good for twice your grace period—in other words, if your grace period is six months, stick with packages that have an expiration date that's at least 12 months away. And, as with all food storage, be sure to rotate through your stockpile constantly, using the oldest items first and replacing them with new, so your stored supplies are never at risk of going stale or rancid.

Storage is easy. Because dry dog and cat food "kibble" is made by the extrusion process (a manufacturing process that exposes it to extreme heat), there should be no "bugs" in the bag before you open it, so all you have to do is make sure it doesn't get invaded after you bring it home. I store my dog's unopened bags of kibble in a tight-lidded, metal garbage can in a cool, dark place away from heat sources (like heater vents, refrigerator or freezer coils, furnaces, ovens, or south-facing exterior walls) and away from direct sunlight; heat will speed up the breakdown process of the food's ingredients and make the expiration date irrelevant. Don't buy bags of kibble that have grease spots on the outside—these are likely to be old or to have been stored improperly, causing the oils to leach through the packaging. If your pet also eats moist, canned food, you may find it more economical to buy it by the case (as long as it won't expire before you can rotate through the whole case). Store the cans in a place where they're protected from heat (away from refrigerators, freezers, furnaces or direct sunlight) and freezing temperatures (if they freeze, the cans may pop their seals). You should also make sure you're stocked up on your pet's regular vitamin-mineral supplement, and whatever medications he or she needs regularly or intermittently throughout the year.

Don't forget to put aside water for your pets, too. The amount will depend on each pet's breed, age, activity level and overall health (dogs with diabetes or kidney ailments, for example, might require two or three times the average daily amount). But here's a rule of thumb for the average, healthy dog or cat: For every 10 pounds of body weight, figure one cup of water per day—this allows for the fact that he may waste some by sloshing and drooling around his bowl. (So if your dog weighs 40 pounds, he'll need four cups of water per day, and if your cat weighs 10 pounds, he'll need one cup of water per day.) Using these formulas, calculate how much water your pets will drink during your grace period, and store it in sealed, cleaned containers away from temperature extremes (if they freeze, the bottles might burst). Be sure to provide fresh water at least twice a day, and wash and wipe out the water bowl each time with a clean cloth or paper towel, to remove the slimy layer created by saliva.

If your cat uses a litter box, remember to stockpile enough kitty litter to cover your grace period. Be sure to get the same brand and type of litter your cat is accustomed to, because cats sometimes will shun the litter box (and, therefore, use "the facilities" elsewhere, like the carpet in the living room) if you switch to an unfamiliar litter.

Chapter 13:
Portable Power and Light

1. Dear Karen: Should I get a generator? If so, how do I know what kind to get?

The sense of autonomy you can get with a generator (your own personal electric plant!) is a great luxury, and in some situations there's just no substitute. Whether or not a generator will be helpful enough to offset the headaches that come with it depends on several factors.

First, where do you live? If you're in an apartment or condo without outdoor balconies, portable generators are pretty much not an option. Why? Fumes, mainly. The exhaust from their motors is every bit as deadly as the exhaust from an automobile. The noise is another issue—most generators are so loud you can't carry on a reasonable conversation if you're within 20 feet. For light-duty, there are smaller generators (about the size of two 6-packs, stacked one on top of the other)—you could accommodate one of these by building a sturdy shelf for it, outside, on a windowsill.

Another problem with generators is fuel: whether they run on gasoline or diesel fuel, in order to carry you through your grace period, you'll need someplace outside to stockpile the stuff, possibly at the peril of yourself and anybody who lives nearby (fire, explosion, leakage and all the consequences therein). If you want ballpark ideas, figure about $250 for a two-outlet, 850-watt, portable gas generator, and up to about $4,000 for one that supplies 15,000 watts. For an idea on how much wattage you'll need, walk through your house with a pencil and notepad, and write down the wattage for each electrical appliance you'll want to run on your generator (this information usually is found on the back of each appliance). Add up the wattage, and multiply by two (your generator will run more efficiently if you only draw about half its power-generating capacity). For examples of typical power requirements for some common household appliances, tools and motors see the table below:

GENERATOR WATTAGE GUIDE

APPLIANCE	RUNNING WATTS
Air conditioner (10k BTU)	2500
Attic fan	400-800
Blender	300
Broiler	1400
Clothes dryer (electric)	5750
Clothes dryer (gas)	700
Coffee maker	1000
Computer & monitor	775
Dehumidifier	500
Dishwasher	500
Freezer	500
Furnace fan	700
Garage door 1/2 hp	600
Hair dryer	1000
Iron	1200
Lamps & lighting	500
Dishwasher	40-200
Microwave oven	800
Radio/stereo	50-200
Refrigerator/freezer	1000
Space heater	1300
Stove element	1500
Sump pump 1/4 hp	400
Sump pump 1/2 hp	600
Tape/CD player	50
Television	350
Toaster	900-1500
Vacuum cleaner	600-1500

APPLIANCE	RUNNING WATTS
Washing machine	1200
Water heater	3500
Water pump 1/2 hp	600
Water pump 1 hp	1200

TOOLS	RUNNING WATTS
Air compressor 1 hp	1000
Air compressor 1-1/2 hp	1600
Air compressor 2 hp	2000
Airless sprayer 3/4 hp	850
Battery charger	120
Concrete vibrator	900-3000
Demolition hammer	1500
Grinder 6'	1500
1 hand drill 1/2"	650
Impact wrench 1/2"	600
Router	1100
Sander, 3x24" belt	1200
Sander, 7" disc	1440
Saw, chain	1000
Saw, 7-1/4" circular	1560
Saw, jig	500
Saw, orbital	300
Saw, radial arm	1200
Saw, reciprocating	500

MOTOR POWER REQUIREMENTS

HORSEPOWER RUNNING	WATTS
1/8	275
1/4	400
1/3	450
1/2	600
3/4	850
1	1000
1-1/2	1600
2	2000
3	3000

These ratings are estimates and should only be used as a rough guide. Confirm the power requirements of each of the items you will run by looking at its information panel. If wattage is not shown, you can calculate it by multiplying the amps times the volts (Amps x Volts = Watts).

You might also want to know that as generators grow in power and price, they also grow in size and weight—the largest ones require either wheels or several very strong people to move them ("portable" is a relative term in the largest models).

If you are planning to get a generator, then I suggest you start shopping as soon as possible. Retailers will try to keep their shops well-stocked in order to profit from increased demand as the "deadline" approaches, but the closer we get to that deadline, the more difficult it will be to find a generator, and the lesser your chances of getting a good price.

Where to get a portable generator? Most hardware stores, The Home Depot, Sears and many proprietary lawn-mower-type shops (e.g., Honda and Kawasaki dealerships) sell them. Or, you can order one through a catalog that sells tools and machinery, such as Northern Tool & Equipment (800-533-5545) or Tek Supply (800-835-7877).

While we're on the subject, there also are built-in generators, which can be direct-wired to your building by a licensed electrician. Figure on several thousand dollars (usually around $8,000 and up) for this machine and the labor to hook it up—the final price on fuel type and size. It looks like a central air conditioning unit, usually set beside the building near your electricity service box, and often enclosed in a custom-built, insulated "house" of its own to muffle the noise and protect it against the elements. The top-of-the-line model is set up to start itself automatically when the regular power supply goes off. Because it's hooked up to the house's wiring, you can continue using designated wall outlets and switches as usual, and if your generator is powerful enough, you can keep your refrigerator and freezer (and furnace) running, too. Once you've bought and paid for your generator, the only hitch is fuel. You have to buy it, store it, and rotate through it regularly so you're sure it's fresh.

2. Dear Karen: I can't (or don't want to) use a portable generator. Any other options for me?

If you only need power to run a few, low-draw appliances such as a reading lamp, a heating pad, or a fish aquarium's filter pump, aerator and tank heater, you might consider getting a small power inverter. These range in size from that of a box of tissues to a 4-slice toaster, and they convert DC (battery) power to 110 AC (the kind of power that's available to you through your standard electric outlets). They can be plugged into your car's cigarette lighter, or, if you buy a set of miniature "jumper cables" that hook it to a battery, you can use them anywhere you have a 12-volt (automobile-type) battery. The smaller ones produce about 100 watts of power and cost as little as $20 (plus the battery, of course); the largest ones about 2,500 watts and cost up to $1000, plus the cost of batteries. Power inverters are available at automotive supply stores, camping, hunting and RV supply stores, variety stores, hardware stores, Sears, computer stores (like Radio Shack), and through home gadget-and-tool-type mail-order catalogs like Brookstone (800-926-7000) and Northern Power and Equipment (800-533-5545). A brand-new 12-volt battery costs from $35 to $75 at automotive supply stores. Depending on the size (wattage) of your power inverter-battery setup, and on how much juice you're drawing from the battery, you can use a power inverter for anywhere from 2 hours to 12 hours—even longer if you don't have to keep it running constantly. You can either get the battery recharged at some location that has power, recharge it by hooking it to your idling vehicle with jumper cables (have an auto mechanic show you how to do this safely), or simply have additional batteries on hand, all charged up and ready to use.

Marine batteries are even better to use for this purpose than automotive batteries, since the former are better able to withstand being completely drained and recharged on a constant basis. It's also possible to purchase a single solar panel that can be used to recharge this battery for long-term use if electrical power is not available.

One word of caution: Even though there's no noisy, smelly

engine driving this setup, you still can't keep a 12-volt battery inside your house, not even for a day. Large batteries emit significant toxic fumes and are a safety risk for explosion, not to mention the risk of severe burns if a pet, child or unwitting adult should accidentally get leaked battery acid on his/her skin. I recommend that if you plan to use a power inverter to run a heating pad or heat lamp or reading light during a crisis, rig up a sturdy shelf to support the battery outside a window, or set it up on a porch or balcony, and run a heavy-duty extension cord into your house from there. Keep at least one 12-volt battery charged up and ready for emergency use in a garage or tool shed.

3. Dear Karen: Can you give me some ideas on how to provide light in a dark house with no electricity?

Rule number one is to avoid using any open flames, such as wax or oil candles, for anything other than just finding your way to the nearest flashlight or lighting the dinner table while you're eating. The fire danger is just too great to use candles for everyday lighting. But there are other options that are not only safer but also provide a much better quality of light—in some cases, good enough to read by. Here are some of the better ones I've found.

● In my opinion, the best "serious" flashlight around is the Craftsman Professional Rechargeable Lantern from Sears. It's expensive (about $50), but it's really bright (like a car's headlight), and it's rechargeable, either by plugging into a standard 110 outlet, or by plugging into a car's cigarette lighter with the adapter that comes with the flashlight. My biggest complaint about these flashlights, aside from their price, used to be that you couldn't replace broken parts—if the bulb burned out, for example, or the battery wore out and wouldn't take a charge, the whole light was worthless. But now you can buy replacement parts at Sears, so it's a good investment. And as flashlights go, you can't beat that bright beam.

● Battery-powered lanterns have really improved a lot over the years—some have two or more fluorescent tubes that put out a lot of light. GE makes some nice battery-powered lanterns that run on four D-size batteries and cost about $10 to $40, depending on size. I found them in a DTE Edison America catalog called "Energy-Related Products for the Home & Family," 800-573-6232.

Check out the camping section in variety and department stores, as well as camping and RV stores, for different brands and configurations of battery-powered lighting. There are wall-mounted, ceiling-mounted, tabletop and hand-held varieties.

● The best lamp that I know of is an Aladdin lamp. It provides that same illumination as a 60-watt bulb. They are also fairly attractive! (They can be purchased from many retailers.)

4. Dear Karen: If I have to rely on flashlights and batteries for very long, I'm going to go broke buying batteries, and I hate the idea of all those used batteries going into the landfill. Are there any other alternatives for good-quality, reliable light sources?

You bet. There are several options.

Oil lanterns are available at most hardware stores and variety stores, along with a variety of colored and scented lamp oils to fuel them. Dietz brand is suitable for indoor or outdoor use and it has a handle for easy transport. For indoor lighting, I highly recommend that you use candle oil instead of lamp oil. A 12-ounce bottle of candle oil costs about $3, compared to $2 for lamp oil, but the extra cost is well worth it because the candle oil is virtually smoke-free and odor free.

A solar-powered lantern is a neat alternative—you can place it in the sunshine to charge during the day, then use it for up to 8 hours at night. I found one in the DTE catalog (800-573-6232) that has a detachable solar module and two fluorescent tubes. It's expensive ($99.98 in the catalog), but a neat idea that could eventually pay for itself in terms of the money you save in not having to purchase batteries.

From the DTE Edison America catalog (800-573-6232), you can get *solar-powered lamps* to light your walkway, driveway, and paths to frequently visited spots (such as an outdoor potty): they're available for mounting on poles, or directly on decks, walls, or any other surface. They shut themselves off automatically at daybreak and are available in sets of two, for $35 to $70 a pair, depending on size and features.

I found a *solar-powered flashlight,* which reportedly gives three hours of operation on a day's charge (I haven't actually tested this particular product). The manufacturer claims it floats and can be used underwater to depths of 60 feet. Available for $30 in the Harmony catalog (800-869-3446).

5. Dear Karen: Do you know of any reliable radio that we can use for entertainment and keeping up with the news, without going through a lot of batteries?

There's an AM-FM radio, called the Sun-Mate, which runs on four different kinds of energy: solar power, regular AC power, two AA batteries, or dynamo power (generated when you wind a built-in crank for 30 seconds, which gives you about two hours of operation). It's durable and lightweight, and costs about $30. I found it in a DTE Edison America catalog called "Energy-Related Products for the Home and Family" (800-573-6232).

If you also want to keep tabs on the National Weather Service broadcasts for approaching storms, I found a battery-powered (two AA batteries), AM/FM weather radio for $45 in the Harmony catalog (800-869-3446).

Chapter 14:
Caring for People with Special Needs

1. Dear Karen: If the government's ability to send out regular payments is affected, what will happen to people who have government-funded placements at residential care facilities, such as nursing homes and mental hospitals?

It is unlikely that government-supported patients will be kicked out onto the street if their accounts aren't paid up-to-date, but here's one way to address the potential for this sort of scenario. If you know someone who lives in such a facility, consider "adopting" them into your life. In other words, take an interest in their care and well-being. Become a regular sight, so the administrators and staff know who you are. Find out what the policy is, if payment for a government-funded inpatient is delayed. If eviction is a real possibility, consider involving your church, local newspaper or TV station, and civic organization. Encourage your community to get involved, possibly even to adopt entire wings of these facilities during the Y2K transition, if necessary, taking up a collection to pay expenses, charitably, with the realization that the government may never pay it back.

2. Dear Karen: If there is no heat and electricity, what will become of the elderly, the disabled, and the ill?

It's up to us, isn't it? As fellow humans, I think it's time we started taking responsibility for making sure our neighbors are cared for, and because you asked this question, I think you're probably in agreement with me. If you live in an apartment in the city, get to know the people in your building. If there's an elderly or disabled resident who can't take the stairs when the elevator stops, make it your responsibility to check in on him or her, invite him or her into your home, share your hot soup, help him or her contact family members, and so forth. By the same token, if you live in a rural or suburban area, take your family or a couple of church members with you to meet with elderly and/or disabled neighbors, and anybody who lives alone. If you can, discuss the Y2K issue with them so they have the opportunity to make preparations of their own, but offer your services to help—you can take them with you when you drive to the nearest buyer's club, or ask for a list of items you can pick up for them, then help them store the stuff, and be prepared to help them in any way you can. Try to get everybody involved in this. For people who simply can't live on their own without the usual conveniences (and if there's no room for them in your own home), you can help them by calling around and finding a place for them to stay, such as another family, or a community shelter. I truly believe there's a silver lining to just about everything that happens, including the Y2K crisis. Wouldn't it be wonderful if it caused us all to become more generous and community-minded? As I see it, the only way we can sail through an experience like this, and come out shining, is to do it together. Whatever it costs you, it will pay you back many times over, in ways you never imagined.

Chapter 15:
Keeping Warm, Keeping Cool

1. Dear Karen: It's hot here year-round, sometimes staying in the 100s for several weeks at a time. How do I keep my family cool?

By all means, let's not forget the millions of people who live in the southern heat! You cold-weather folks may laugh, but it's no joke—the heat can be really hard on everybody, especially the elderly, the very young, those who do manual labor, those who are ill or disabled, and anybody who can't get out of the heat (including pets). Without electricity to run air conditioners, a lot of folks will be in a world of hurt when the mercury goes up and stays there. Here are some tips that can help keep you and your loved ones more comfortable.

- Encourage everyone to drink lots of water throughout the day. When your body is well-hydrated, it is better able to cool itself. This is true of family pets as well—make sure their water source is clean, fresh, and readily available.
- Stay out of the direct sun whenever possible, and wear a wide-brimmed hat to create your own portable shade. Be sure to provide shade for your pets, too.
- Whenever possible, limit strenuous work and play to the cooler times of the day.
- Learn how different bodies cool themselves. Humans and horses cool primarily through sweating and the cooling reaction that takes place on the skin when sweat evaporates, so get yourself (and the backyard horse) wet or damp, then stand in a

breeze to encourage evaporation (it doesn't require a lot of water—just a wet cloth swiped over the skin can work wonders). If there's precious little breeze, a brisk rubdown with witch hazel will cool you (or your horse) even faster than water, because it has a tendency to evaporate faster. (Rubbing alcohol also works, but it is very drying and can irritate sensitive skin.) The witch hazel trick can work wonders for the elderly or the ill, and it'll help people sleep when it's sweltering at night. Dogs cool themselves primarily by panting, and by lying against a cool surface, to which they can transfer some of their extra body heat. If your dog likes playing in water, he might enjoy a plastic wading pool with an inch or two of water in it—a lot of dogs will jump right in and lie down in the shallow water. Cats are very inefficient at cooling off and will benefit mainly from lying on a cool surface, which can absorb some of their body heat. If a cat becomes overheated enough to pant, he's potentially in serious trouble and should be dunked up to his neck—do this quickly, without a lot of fanfare, so he doesn't have time to panic. (And make sure you're holding your cat securely, so he or she can't bite or scratch you. Ask your vet or groom for advice ahead of time, so you can learn how to hold your cat for "scary" procedures like this.)

2. Dear Karen: It's bitterly cold here in the winter, sometimes staying below 0° F for several weeks at a time. How do I keep my family warm?

If you don't have a fireplace or a wood stove, don't despair: there might be some good options for you. First and foremost, as soon as you're aware that you're without heat, you can take steps to keep the heat that's already in your house from escaping. Close the shades, blinds and drapes. If your window coverings are flimsy, or if you have windows that don't have any coverings, cover them with blankets or quilts (you can affix them to the window frame with tacks and a tack hammer, or drape them over a telescoping shower rod fitted into the window frame). Close off any parts of the house that you won't be using, such as extra bedrooms, a formal dining room, and so forth. In fact, it might be wise to move your family and all eating, leisure and sleeping activities to one or two rooms in the house and close off everything else to concentrate the warmth.

For safety's sake, you must be very choosy about any supplemental heating devices you bring into the house. Lots of people are under the mistaken impression that all kerosene, diesel, propane and waste-oil space heaters are safe indoors as long as you keep a window ajar, to let toxic fumes out and fresh air in. Not so, say several folks-in-the-know. Most fuel-burning space heaters were meant to be used in workshops and open garages, where the "ventilation" consists of a gaping garage door and a total lack of insulation. The fumes they emit are sufficiently deadly that they could make the air in an enclosed room uniformly toxic, or create toxic "pockets" interspersed with only thin veins of fresh air wafting in from the open window. If the open window is allowing a breeze to come in, which might create enough turbulence to break up the toxic pockets, the result is not "safe air"; rather, you've only partially diluted the toxins. And don't be confused by the variety of methods used to express the heat—whether the heater has an open flame, a glowing element, an infrared dish or quartz elements, if it's powered by combustible fuel (kerosene, white gas, No. 2 heating oil, diesel or propane), it is not safe in your house unless it's either built-in with an approved venting system, or is rated 99% efficient.

However, from what I've heard, the best and safest home heater is a kerosene space heater that you can get at your local home improvement or hardware store.

So, before you buy, be sure to study the pamphlet that comes with the heater: if it specifically states that it's a "vent-free" heater, with an efficiency of "99% or greater," "safe to use indoors," then it should be safe for your family as long as you follow instructions to the letter and are very careful to prevent tipovers. Otherwise, if the label or accompanying pamphlet contains language such as, "great for keeping a campsite or job-site warm," or "can heat an area the size of a two-car garage," pass it by—if it were safe for in-the-house use, this information would be clearly, proudly stated.

No matter how safe a label says a fuel-burning heater is, don't take chances. If you buy the heater, spend a little more and buy a smoke detector and a battery-powered carbon monoxide detector, too (they're usually in the same aisle as the smoke detectors). On the first day of every month, make sure the detectors are operating properly, and change the batteries every year, whether they need it or not.

Electric space heaters can be another option. Because they're limited to 1500 watts or less by the Underwriters Laboratory, it can be reasonable to power them with either a generator or a power inverter hooked to one or more 12-volt batteries. Be advised that many space heaters contain elements or reflective dishes that are coated with Teflon™ or other materials that are known to emit toxic fumes when heated. For humans and larger pets such as dogs and even cats, the level of fumes is not likely to cause problems (that we know of!). For more sensitive creatures, such as caged birds and other exotics, they can be quickly deadly. So, before you buy, study the specifications. If any of the heated parts are coated with a material that resembles what's on non-stick cookware, you'd better pass it by.

The use of a generator or power inverter to run an electric space heater becomes more and more feasible if other factors permit you to shut the supplemental heaters down for at least 50% of the time. For example, if everybody in the family can get up, out, and moving enough to warm up their own inner cores during the daytime, that's a real plus. If everybody has lots of layers of insulating clothing, such as Polar Fleece, wool, and silk, make sure they're being worn, and if they get wet make sure they're replaced with dry. Make sure everybody has a sleeping bag rated to keep campers warm in temperatures far colder than what's considered extreme in your area, and make sure everybody has sleepwear that's optimally warm without being restrictive so they're able to sleep comfortably, without fighting with twisted, binding PJs (it's impossible to keep warm if you're always tired from not getting a good night's sleep).

And don't forget about good, old-fashioned long underwear! Layering is still an obvious but effective technique for keeping warm.

And, finally, if the cold weather is severe and your living situation simply does not lend itself to "primitive" methods of keeping warm (or if one or more members of your family is disabled or otherwise unable to tolerate the cold), then you must have a contingency plan in place. Do some investigating now, before the need arises. Find a local church or community gathering place, where there's a heat source, or where the community plans to have a generator for adequate heat, plus beds, blankets, food, water, toilets, showers, etc., for people who will need to relocate during a crisis. Or, arrange ahead of time to move in with a family member or a friend in the event of a prolonged power outage.

Even better, if you are prepared you can open your home to others in need.

Chapter 16:
Home Decorating for Y2K

On a lighter note, I recently was written up in an article on Y2K for the *Dallas Observer*. It was basically a fair article, but one of the things I found hysterical was the caption under my picture. It read that I "advise women on how to prepare for Y2K with an eye for fashion."

How did the writer get that? I guess that came from my Website, where I said that you didn't have to decorate your house in olive drab, and I could give Martha Stewart a run for her money!

Please . . . do I look like the Martha Stewart of Y2K??? Gift-wrapped food storage . . . how to make water effervescent for a post-Y2K dinner party . . . decorating your root cellar . . . setting the perfect Y2K table (dinner napkins folded into little buckets at each place setting) . . . choosing the right buckets for your decor (multipurpose latrine and bookshelves). . . . I had to laugh!

However, in response I issued a challenge on my Website: "Do you have any Y2K-preparedness decorating ideas you want to share?" Step aside Martha . . . here we come!

These were the top winners of the "Y2K-Martha Stewart" Contest!

Winner #1: Decorating Tips
Dear Karen,

For simple yet delightful living room storage, you can place trash cans at either end of the couch, top with round pieces of plywood, and store your extra dry goods inside. This makes a lovely lamp table, especially if you use a mylar emergency blanket as a tablecloth. Simply lovely!!

Cover your 50-lb. bags of beans in tailored pillow cases (stripes trimmed with buttons for that nautical look, you know) and place at the head of your bed for a lovely backrest.

A five-gallon bucket topped with a pretty sheet makes a fine footstool or extra seat. Gather the fabric around the top and tie with dental floss, and you will have both bedding and clean teeth later.

Enjoy! Tracey

[KA: This does sound so Martha-ish!]

Winner #2: Humor

Dear Karen,

I don't know if this actually meets the criteria for your challenge, but I needed a laugh and a lighter look at things. If nothing else . . . enjoy! (BTW . . . it is completely tongue-in-cheek!)

Ladies, in the midst of our preparations for surviving the chaos of the new millennium, we must be ever aware of how we appear to others and the image we project. How else can we be taken seriously and emulated to the fullest extent? I began my personal journey in this by replacing my entire wardrobe with items created from old military uniforms. I created a lovely seasonal wardrobe (we don't know how long this will last after all!) consisting of forest-garb, desert cammies, and arctic-wear. Personally I think the full length evening dress of arctic grays and whites I created in my spare time (I just completed canning every piece of fruit in the state of Colorado single-handedly this past weekend so I have been pressed for time) is the prettiest seen thus far. It will be so special for those holiday get-togethers over the kerosene heater and is durable enough to withstand carrying logs for the fireplace. A hostess must be both a delight to the eye as well as maintain a practical aspect.

Now back to decorating ideas . . . our hay bale home lends itself nicely to a harvest theme. By just adding small accents like flowers you can give the whole house a lift in the spring. I have also found that simply covering a 50-gallon water container with a delightful little cloth allows it to function as a table or lamp stand. And did you know that if you group six 10-lb. cans together and tie them with cording they serve quite nicely as an ottoman? You may wish to add fabric to coordinate with the entire room. In a pinch, the bags that large quantities of rice, grain, etc., come in, can serve as covers with that "down-home" look. How rustic! Another cute idea I have come up with is to replace our furniture with these bags, while they are still full! Large piles of the grain bags can be arranged in a variety of ways to serve your needs for family living as well as entertaining at anytime! Just be creative! Be sure to back the pieces up to a wall though as they may tip over until you adjust to sitting on this new style of sofa and chair!

We are all sure to have large quantities of candles lying about and this will add to the ambiance of your home. It will also reduce the chances of people seeing dirt and dust which will significantly increase without the use of our vacuums! And the time saved in not vacuuming can easily be utilized in creating a textured look to your walls with egg cartons! That's right! Simply staple, nail, or glue the cartons directly to your walls for added insulation!

Need to have more people sharing smaller spaces to conserve heat but still want to provide privacy? Easy enough! Stack those extra cans of food up as divider walls in any configuration you desire! (A word of caution though for those with toddlers: these walls are not solid, and you may have to recreate your dividers a few times!)

Ladies, the ideas are limitless. Don't wait to get started . . . the crisis may not last long enough for us to try everything we come up with! Let your mind and hands experiment and soon you will find yourselves being the trend setters of the decorator world!

Trish

Winner #3: Shower

Dear Karen,

I've just read your letter about the contest on "Y2K preparedness decorating ideas." I got an idea just yesterday morning on my way to church. As my husband and I were driving (not at the same time), we passed through wooded areas and cotton fields near the river. There are deer stands in the area. And one that I saw was camouflaged and had a cone top on it. I thought wouldn't that be a great way for men and women to keep their privacy while bathing (showering, actually). You could place a camouflage net around the open area like a shower curtain. And if more privacy were needed, I suppose you could hang up an actual shower curtain. But the fact is that it is a trustworthy stand used by hunters every year, and it is well-hidden by its camo colors.

God bless you! Bernadette

[I'd just use caution bathing during hunting season! K]

Winner #4: Humor

Dear Karen,

I was shocked that you have not considered the ramifications of not being prepared, fashionably speaking, for Y2K. Mind you, I have two children, and they do come in a close second to decorating and fashion. I mean, really, what mother in her right mind would allow a child to go through this ordeal feeling less than fashionable?

The first thing all mothers should worry about is fashion. The hairstyle is easy and ever so savvy. It is so universal that you can use the same principle for you, your husband, sons and daughters. It is, however, imperative that you stock up on styling gel. By the way, you inadvertently left that off of your list. Rather than worry that you may not be able to wash your hair on a daily basis, just rub in the styling gel and go. No one will ever know that you have not washed your hair for weeks AND you will be in style.

As for clothes, this is your opportunity to take the "grunge" look to the extreme, with class and elegance, of course. In order to achieve this, you must begin buying your clothes several sizes bigger, just make sure you don't forget to buy matching belts and scarves. It is also important that you buy prints and not solids. By doing so, one cannot tell if your garment is dirty or if that is the pattern! How practical!

During this difficult time we must not forget to accessorize. A nice pearl necklace can dress up any outfit. Ladies, this is your chance to let your hair down (if you have water to wash it and it is not glued to your head). You can bet that fashion is on the top of every woman's list, so don't be left out!

In your frenzy to rush out and prepare your wardrobe, let's not forget about your house. Think of all the people who may have to come to your house to stay until their power or water is back on.

Imagine if you didn't take the time to decorate. How embarrassing would that be? You would be mud in all of the social circles.

The one item that no woman ever wants to be without is toilet paper. What a decorating phenomenon! Who needs crepe paper for those parties??? Just string toilet paper around the room, make some streamers, and you have a wonderfully practical decoration.

Another tip for ambiance in a room, don't waste your time buying scarves to drape over those lamp shades, use panties or dishtowels that need drying. You still achieve that soft light and you dry your laundry (assuming you have electricity to power the lamp). CAUTION: don't try this with oil lamps.

Oh, Karen, thanks so much for all of the time and energy you have put into this Website, but don't you think it's time to move on to more important things??? Where has your mind been not to think about these things? We wouldn't want to let our children down by not giving them that fashion advantage, would we? After all, what kind of mothers would that make us?

Wendy W.

Winner #5: Humor

Dear Karen,

As the new millennium approaches women everywhere are concerned with what the latest styles in decorating and high fashion will be. Don't despair. You can be the epitome of haute couture for very little cost, using what you have on hand. The emphasis will be on practicality as well as eye-catching appeal.

Stack boxes or buckets of food in groupings at the end of your sofa and beside your chairs, to end table height. Drape with a colorful blanket, or better yet one of those metallic blankets, and top with your favorite kerosene lantern. Several boxes side by side make a great coffee table. A great place for displaying your survival books.

Stack those 50-gallon drums of water in a corner of your porch and display your favorite plants on them. Milk jugs or soda jugs full of water can be painted to add a touch of color and artfully displayed all around your home. Medical supplies such as scalpels, hemostats, thermometers, blood pressure cuff, and stethoscope can be hung on a mobile. Display your bandages and healing ointments in a shadow box.

Remember the pictures of roosters people used to make with beans, corn, etc.? Well, that's sure to come back in style so start yours now. You can always eat your picture later. And don't forget your ammo. Bullets can be arranged into the most wonderful picture shapes. That way they are also handy if you want to go hunting.

Macaroni necklaces, bracelets and ear rings are what the smartly dressed woman will be wearing in the new millennium. Herbs can be twisted into ropes or bracelets and will be very much in demand as they are harder to make. Sort of a meal on a string.

Get started now, and you can be the envy of every woman in your neighborhood.

[KA: I thought the idea of eating your pictures was hysterical!]

Winner # 6

Dear Karen,

I've always felt the need to prepare for possible "changes" that could cause the family distress. Several of the things I do, most visitors look at as "nice" decorating ideas . . . never realizing the "real" reason for them.

Some of my favorites are:

● Window quilts. These are hand-quilted (machine would be nice, too—never got the hang of it) quilts that are just a bit bigger than the windows you need to cover to keep the heat in. When the sun goes down, the window quilts are dropped into place. We use a big one to cover French doors on the north side of our home. Made it with two big pieces of ecru muslin, a thin quilt batting, with a survival (reflective) blanket sandwiched inside if you wish.

● Storing #10 cans under the bed can make it look as though you spent a lot of money to have a "raised" bed.

● Small barrels look just like the round decorator tables once you put a skirt and glass top on them.

● The back of your clothes closet is a good place to store #10 cans and paper goods. All of these places are out of sight but very readily accessible.

● For an interesting child's table you can use a small barrel as the base, and an inexpensive piece of plywood as the top. Five-gallon buckets make nice stools. You might cover the sides with contact paper, wallpaper or even paint. You can make cushions for the top if you wish. Some stores even sell cushions (to be used on kitchen stools) that work nicely if you're not into sewing. An added bonus to using buckets as chairs is that when full they are too heavy for most children to move. This is really handy if you have children who like to use chairs to get into things that you are trying to keep out of their reach.

● For a quick and easy to store one burner stove you can make a "buddy burner." I learned this in Girl Scouts years ago and have used them many, many times during power outages due to ice storms and such. I can fix coffee and then feed the kids just as quickly as any other morning with just three of these. I can think of few things worse than a morning without coffee and hungry screaming kids. It makes me cringe to just think about it! I am NOT a morning person!

● For great instructions dig out your old G.S. handbook, buy one (they still have several other great survival/camping ideas) or check one out of the library. I'll try and give a general outline here. The burner is made by coiling cardboard strips the same width as the sides of a tuna can tightly inside a tuna can. Carefully pour melted paraffin over the coils and into the can. Don't touch until it has cooled. Save the tuna lid. Poke two holes in it about one inch apart close to one edge. Attach a 12-inch piece of wire coat hanger through the holes in the lid. It will look like a flat frying pan. This is what you use to control the flame on the burner. Then the cooktop is made from a juice can (Hawaiian Punch size) or even a #10 can from which one end has been removed. Using tin snips, cut an opening big enough to slide the tuna/burner through when the open end is placed on a heat proof surface. I use a grill that I place over my regular stove burners. You will need to use a can opener or a punch to put a few holes near the top (closed end) of the cooktop for ventilation. I just use my smaller regular pans on the top. I've seen others put a little butter on the top of the can/cooktop and fry an egg on the top of the can. No pans! You can also heat an open can of Spaghetti-O's right on top of the cooktop. When you are done, use the tuna lid to smother the flame. I've been able to use these buddy burners for several meals before retiring them to the trash.

● A window seat or behind the sofa table can be made by using boxes of stored goods. Simply cover with coordinating fabric and a piece of glass or wood for the table, or a cushion for the window seat. Nobody will ever know what is under the lovely tablecloth unless you tell them.

These are a few of my favorite ways of storing, conserving space and quickly cooking a meal. I hope they can help others as they try and find "just one more place" to put things, and survive in comfort and peace.

No Matter What . . . Keep Your Sense of Humor!

The Proverbs 31 Woman

The Proverbs 31 Woman rises hours before her family so she can press their clothes, artfully apply her make-up and fix them a hot breakfast. She bakes a batch of brownies for the school carnival and then spends quiet time with the Lord so she can cheerfully wake her family to the new day. She designs and sews the costumes for the church pageant, offers encouragement and homemade cookies to the neighbors and co-workers. She drives across town to take advantage of the freshest produce at the lowest prices and then rushes home so she can greet her husband with a smile and a kiss. They gather around the table for another gourmet meal as her husband and children shower her with praise. Afterward, they all sit around the fireplace for family devotions before she tucks her children into bed.

She sings them a song, kisses their sweet faces and then goes into the den to rub her husband's shoulders. Finally, she slips into her Victoria's Secret lace gown and slides into her satin sheets. She falls asleep with a smile on her face just thinking about tomorrow and the joy it will bring.

The Proverbs 31 Woman—in Progress

She wakes up late because her two-year-old dropped the alarm clock in the toilet. No time to iron her husband's shirt so she hangs it up in the bathroom and tells him the steam from his shower will take out the wrinkles. Breakfast consists of a pop tart. If they want a hot breakfast they can put it in the toaster. Her child reminds her he needs two dozen brownies for the school carnival, no time to bake so she sticks a bow on Aunt Mabel's fruitcake and assures him fruitcake is a favorite at carnivals! Morning devotions consist of "Lord, please let me get the kids to the bus stop on time." The church play is tonight and still no costume, so she rips the Mickey Mouse sheet from the bed and wraps it around her son's head. "Of course you look like a Shepherd Billy! And mice were plentiful in the Bible days." She realizes it's already Wednesday and her Community Bible Study lesson isn't even started. "I'll do it tonight after the kids are in bed" she thinks. She quickly puts some frozen TV dinners in the oven only to hear the doorbell ring and suddenly remembers tonight is the night she invited the new neighbors for dinner.

When she finally gets her children tucked into bed, she prays for them, tells them their favorite "Daniel and the Lion's Den" story for the 22nd time in a row, kisses their sweet faces as her little one places his hands on her face and says in his most angelic little voice, "Mommy?" "Yes sweetie?" "What's that green thing on your tooth?" She goes through the house and straightens it the best she can, slips into her T-shirt and sweats and slides into bed next to her sleeping husband. She opens her Bible and falls asleep before the first line is read.

(This came to me via email so I don't have a copyright. If anyone knows where it came from, I'd love to know so I could give credit.)

The Busy Woman's Y2K Home Preparedness Check List

CHECK LIST ITEMS	NUMBER OF MONTHS		
	1	6	12+

Kitchen
PANTRY
Variety of Beans
- Great Northern ☐ ☐ ☐
- Kidney beans ☐ ☐ ☐
- Lentils ☐ ☐ ☐
- Navy ☐ ☐ ☐
- Pinto ☐ ☐ ☐
- Red beans ☐ ☐ ☐
- Sprouting peas, etc. ☐ ☐ ☐

Rice and Grains
- Barley ☐ ☐ ☐
- Cold cereals ☐ ☐ ☐
- Corn (popcorn and field corn) ☐ ☐ ☐
- Flour (Wheat, white and other varieties) ☐ ☐ ☐
- Instant hot cereals (oatmeal, cream of wheat, etc.) ☐ ☐ ☐
- Oatmeal ☐ ☐ ☐
- Rice (brown, white, or combination) ☐ ☐ ☐

Meat and Fish
- Chicken ☐ ☐ ☐
- Corned beef ☐ ☐ ☐
- Salmon ☐ ☐ ☐
- Soy protein—Taco filling, BBQ beef, etc. ☐ ☐ ☐
- Spam ☐ ☐ ☐
- Tuna ☐ ☐ ☐

Oil (Cooking Agents)
- Baking powder ☐ ☐ ☐
- Baking soda ☐ ☐ ☐

CHECK LIST ITEMS	NUMBER OF MONTHS		
	1	6	12+
● Oils	❏	❏	❏
● Butter flavored Crisco	❏	❏	❏
● Shortening (like Crisco)	❏	❏	❏
● Olive oil (stores best)	❏	❏	❏
● Vegetable oil (canola stores well)	❏	❏	❏
● Mayonnaise (small jars if there is no refrigeration)	❏	❏	❏
● Yeast (in a pinch you can use sourdough)	❏	❏	❏
Salt			
● Iodized	❏	❏	❏
● Rock salt	❏	❏	❏
● Sea salt	❏	❏	❏
Sugar (Sweeteners)			
● Brown sugar	❏	❏	❏
● Corn syrup	❏	❏	❏
● Equal or Sweet N'Low (just to have on hand for us diehards!)	❏	❏	❏
● Honey	❏	❏	❏
● Maple syrup	❏	❏	❏
● Molasses	❏	❏	❏
● Powdered sugar	❏	❏	❏
● White sugar	❏	❏	❏
Pasta			
● Macaroni	❏	❏	❏
● Shells	❏	❏	❏
● Spaghetti (with jars of heat-up sauce)	❏	❏	❏
Dairy Products			
● Dry buttermilk	❏	❏	❏
● Milk (canned evaporated)	❏	❏	❏
● Parmesan cheese	❏	❏	❏
● Powdered butter/margarine is available (like Butter Busters)	❏	❏	❏
● Cheese powder (This sounded gross to	❏	❏	❏

CHECK LIST ITEMS	NUMBER OF MONTHS		
	1	6	12+

me until I realized it was what was in the boxes of prepared Macaroni & Cheese!)

Eggs
- Powdered eggs ❑ ❑ ❑

Vegetables
- Dehydrated vegetables ❑ ❑ ❑
- Beets ❑ ❑ ❑
- Broccoli ❑ ❑ ❑
- Cabbage ❑ ❑ ❑
- Canned and bottled vegetables ❑ ❑ ❑
- Carrots ❑ ❑ ❑
- Celery ❑ ❑ ❑
- Creamed corn ❑ ❑ ❑
- Green beans ❑ ❑ ❑
- Instant mashed potatoes ❑ ❑ ❑
- Peas ❑ ❑ ❑
- Soup and stew blends ❑ ❑ ❑
- Spinach ❑ ❑ ❑

Fruits
- Apples ❑ ❑ ❑
- Applesauce ❑ ❑ ❑
- Apricots ❑ ❑ ❑
- Bananas ❑ ❑ ❑
- Canned and bottled fruit juices ❑ ❑ ❑
- Flavored apples ❑ ❑ ❑
- Fruit cocktail ❑ ❑ ❑
- Lemon juice ❑ ❑ ❑
  (bottled does not have to be refrigerated)
- Oranges ❑ ❑ ❑
- Peaches ❑ ❑ ❑
- Raisins ❑ ❑ ❑
- Small boxes of juice for kids ❑ ❑ ❑
- Variety of dehydrated fruits ❑ ❑ ❑

CHECK LIST ITEMS	NUMBER OF MONTHS		
	1	6	12+

Soups
- Canned chicken/beef stock   ❑ ❑ ❑
- Cream of mushroom, broccoli, etc.   ❑ ❑ ❑
- Soup starter   ❑ ❑ ❑
- Variety of canned soups   ❑ ❑ ❑
  (Chicken Noodle, Tomato, etc.)
- Vegetable soups   ❑ ❑ ❑

Spices and Flavorings
- Baking cocoa   ❑ ❑ ❑
- Basil   ❑ ❑ ❑
- Bouillon (beef and chicken)   ❑ ❑ ❑
- Canned tomatoes   ❑ ❑ ❑
- Chili powder   ❑ ❑ ❑
- Cinnamon   ❑ ❑ ❑
- Garlic (powder, minced, salt)   ❑ ❑ ❑
- Green peppers   ❑ ❑ ❑
- Ketchup (Tomato products are a regular   ❑ ❑ ❑
  in most American kids' diets and they will
  often eat things with ketchup on them they
  wouldn't otherwise! Ketchup is high in
  sugar and kids are almost addicted to it!)
- Mustard   ❑ ❑ ❑
- Onions (powder, flakes, salt)   ❑ ❑ ❑
- Oregano   ❑ ❑ ❑
- Pepper   ❑ ❑ ❑
- Salad dressing   ❑ ❑ ❑
- Salsa   ❑ ❑ ❑
- Soy sauce   ❑ ❑ ❑
- Teriyaki sauce   ❑ ❑ ❑
- Tomato paste   ❑ ❑ ❑
- Tomato powder   ❑ ❑ ❑
- Tomato sauce   ❑ ❑ ❑
- Vinegar (plain and flavored)   ❑ ❑ ❑
- Worcestershire sauce   ❑ ❑ ❑
- Bay leaves   ❑ ❑ ❑
  (I've found bay leaves are great for keep-

CHECK LIST ITEMS	NUMBER OF MONTHS		
	1	6	12+

ing bugs out of flour and cereal so you
might want to get an extra large bottle!)

	1	6	12+
● Seeds for sprouting: (essential for vitamins)	❑	❑	❑
● Alfalfa, mung, radish, sprouting peas, lentils, etc.	❑	❑	❑

Fresh Root Vegetables

	1	6	12+
● Butternut squash	❑	❑	❑
● Potatoes (kept in cool, dark place)	❑	❑	❑
● Waxed rutabagas	❑	❑	❑

Odds and Ends

	1	6	12+
● Biscuit mix	❑	❑	❑
● Canned mushrooms	❑	❑	❑
● Cans of nuts (peanuts, cashews, etc.)	❑	❑	❑
● Cereals	❑	❑	❑
● Crackers	❑	❑	❑
● Pancake mix	❑	❑	❑
● Pickles	❑	❑	❑
● Salad dressing mix (Italian, Ranch—Good Seasons type)	❑	❑	❑
● Waffle mix	❑	❑	❑

Beverages

	1	6	12+
● Coffee (vacuum sealed but already ground if there is a problem with electricity)	❑	❑	❑
● Gatorade	❑	❑	❑
● Hot Chocolate	❑	❑	❑
● Individual coffee bags	❑	❑	❑
● Instant coffee	❑	❑	❑
● Non-carbonated drink mix like Tang, Kool-Aid, etc.)	❑	❑	❑
● Non-dairy creamer	❑	❑	❑
● Sodas (I have lots of friends who say they won't survive without Diet Coke!)	❑	❑	❑
● Tea	❑	❑	❑

CHECK LIST ITEMS	NUMBER OF MONTHS		
	1	6	12+
● Wine in boxes with mylar bags	❑	❑	❑
Quick and Easy to Prepare Foods			
● Canned chili, canned soups, canned meats, peanut butter, etc.	❑	❑	❑
● Freeze or dried or no cook foods	❑	❑	❑
● Instant soups (like Ramon or any soup that you just add water)	❑	❑	❑
● Macaroni and cheese	❑	❑	❑
● Spaghetti sauce	❑	❑	❑
Psychological Foods or Comfort Foods			
● Brownie mixes	❑	❑	❑
● Cake mixes	❑	❑	❑
● Cheerios	❑	❑	❑
● Chocolate chips	❑	❑	❑
● Chocolate milk mix	❑	❑	❑
● Crackers	❑	❑	❑
● Dream Whip	❑	❑	❑
● Hard candies	❑	❑	❑
● Jell-O	❑	❑	❑
● Jelly	❑	❑	❑
● Popcorn	❑	❑	❑
● Powdered drinks (with added vitamin C like Tang)	❑	❑	❑
● Puddings	❑	❑	❑
Baby Food and Formula (Note: I absolutely encourage breast feeding! However, if a woman is in a crisis, it is very possible for her not to have an adequate milk supply. Supplementation may be necessary!)			
● Powdered formula (A pediatrician I spoke with said canned formula wouldn't last as long and was more expensive. Have some bottles of sterile water on hand to mix with the formula.)	❑	❑	❑

CHECK LIST ITEMS	NUMBER OF MONTHS		
	1	**6**	**12+**
● Pureed fruits and vegetables	❑	❑	❑
● Hand grinder to puree table food	❑	❑	❑

Vitamins
- Children's liquid or chewable vitamins ❑ ❑ ❑
- Liquid dietary supplement (like Ensure) ❑ ❑ ❑
- Mineral supplements (like calcium) ❑ ❑ ❑
- Multi-vitamins ❑ ❑ ❑
- Vitamin C ❑ ❑ ❑

Water
- Drinking water ❑ ❑ ❑
- Distilled water ❑ ❑ ❑
- Soda water ❑ ❑ ❑
- Water for cleaning and bathing ❑ ❑ ❑

Remember, as James Stevens says,
"Buy what you eat and eat what you buy."

CUPBOARDS
Cooking Utensils
- French press coffee pot
  (the kind you add hot water to,
  let it steep and then press the
  grounds down) ❑ ❑ ❑
- Solar oven ❑ ❑ ❑
- Wood stove ❑ ❑ ❑
- Gas grill ❑ ❑ ❑
- Camping stove ❑ ❑ ❑
- Pressure cooker ❑ ❑ ❑
- Kettle ❑ ❑ ❑
- Cast iron cookware ❑ ❑ ❑
- Skillet ❑ ❑ ❑
- Dutch oven ❑ ❑ ❑
- Bread pans ❑ ❑ ❑
- Waffle iron ❑ ❑ ❑

CHECK LIST ITEMS	NUMBER OF MONTHS		
	1	6	12+
● Griddle	❑	❑	❑
● Wok	❑	❑	❑
● Plastic storage containers	❑	❑	❑

Under the Sink Stuff

	1	6	12+
● Bleach	❑	❑	❑
● Dishwashing detergent (anti-bacterial)	❑	❑	❑
● Dishpan	❑	❑	❑
● Drying rack	❑	❑	❑
● Dishtowels	❑	❑	❑
● Hand soap (anti-bacterial)	❑	❑	❑
● Hand soap (waterless)	❑	❑	❑
● Sponges	❑	❑	❑
● Steel wool pads (Brillo)	❑	❑	❑
● Rubber gloves	❑	❑	❑
● Cleanser with bleach	❑	❑	❑

Trash Bags

	1	6	12+
● Drawstring, white, tall kitchen bags	❑	❑	❑
● Black garbage bags	❑	❑	❑
● Twisties	❑	❑	❑

Baggies (zip lock)

	1	6	12+
● Small	❑	❑	❑
● Sandwich size	❑	❑	❑
● Large	❑	❑	❑
● Thick freezer bags	❑	❑	❑
● Aluminum foil (various sizes)	❑	❑	❑
● Plastic wrap	❑	❑	❑
● Paper towels	❑	❑	❑
● Paper napkins	❑	❑	❑
● Rags	❑	❑	❑
● Water filters	❑	❑	❑
● Water purifiers	❑	❑	❑
● Iodine	❑	❑	❑
● Manual can opener	❑	❑	❑
(Good Grips are pretty easy)			

CHECK LIST ITEMS	NUMBER OF MONTHS		
	1	6	12+

- Knife sharpener   ❑   ❑   ❑
- Kitchen matches   ❑   ❑   ❑
  (in waterproof container)
- Fire extinguisher   ❑   ❑   ❑

Laundry Room

- Detergent (liquid laundry soap)   ❑   ❑   ❑
- Bleach   ❑   ❑   ❑
- Drying rack   ❑   ❑   ❑
- Clothes line   ❑   ❑   ❑
- Clothes pins   ❑   ❑   ❑
- Washtub   ❑   ❑   ❑
- Buckets   ❑   ❑   ❑
- Dust cloths   ❑   ❑   ❑
- Furniture polish   ❑   ❑   ❑
- Window cleaner   ❑   ❑   ❑
- Light bulbs   ❑   ❑   ❑
- Batteries   ❑   ❑   ❑
- Battery recharger   ❑   ❑   ❑
- Candles   ❑   ❑   ❑
- Matches   ❑   ❑   ❑
- Light sticks   ❑   ❑   ❑
- Oil lamp   ❑   ❑   ❑
- Oil, wicks   ❑   ❑   ❑
- Disinfectant (Lysol)   ❑   ❑   ❑
- Broom   ❑   ❑   ❑
- Air freshener   ❑   ❑   ❑
- Toilet bowl cleaner   ❑   ❑   ❑
- Plunger   ❑   ❑   ❑
- Drain snake   ❑   ❑   ❑
- Drain unclogger (like Drano)   ❑   ❑   ❑

Sewing Kit

- Needles   ❑   ❑   ❑
- Thread   ❑   ❑   ❑
- Scissors   ❑   ❑   ❑

CHECK LIST ITEMS	NUMBER OF MONTHS		
	1	6	12+
● Material	❑	❑	❑

Bathroom

Shower and Tub

	1	6	12+
● Bubble bath (!)	❑	❑	❑
● Bath soap	❑	❑	❑
● Outdoor solar shower bag	❑	❑	❑
● Razor and blades	❑	❑	❑
● Shampoo/conditioner	❑	❑	❑
● Shaving cream	❑	❑	❑
● Tissues	❑	❑	❑
● Toilet paper	❑	❑	❑
● Moist towelettes or baby wipes	❑	❑	❑
● Air freshener	❑	❑	❑

Feminine Hygiene

	1	6	12+
● Maxi Pads	❑	❑	❑
● Tampons	❑	❑	❑
● Panty Liners	❑	❑	❑
● Menstrual Cup (The Keeper) 1-888-882-1818 ext. 30	❑	❑	❑
● Washable pads	❑	❑	❑

Hair Care

	1	6	12+
● Hair brushes	❑	❑	❑
● Combs	❑	❑	❑
● Elastics and ribbons for little girls	❑	❑	❑
● Non-electric curlers (like the little Velcro kind)	❑	❑	❑
● Curling iron (propane)	❑	❑	❑
● Hair cutting scissors	❑	❑	❑

Dental Care

	1	6	12+
● Toothbrushes	❑	❑	❑
● Toothpaste	❑	❑	❑
● Mouthwash	❑	❑	❑

CHECK LIST ITEMS	NUMBER OF MONTHS		
	1	6	12+
● Dental floss	☐	☐	☐
● Denture care products	☐	☐	☐
● Adhesive	☐	☐	☐
● Cleanser	☐	☐	☐

Eye Care

	1	6	12+
● Extra glasses	☐	☐	☐
● Extra replacement screws	☐	☐	☐
● Extra contacts	☐	☐	☐
● Saline solution	☐	☐	☐

Make-up

Don't discount this as unimportant! If wearing make-up is part of your lifestyle, make sure you include enough to last you for awhile. It's important to feel good about how you look! It helps your self-esteem, which will help your family.

	1	6	12+
● Cleanser	☐	☐	☐
● Toner	☐	☐	☐
● Moisturizer	☐	☐	☐
● Foundation	☐	☐	☐
● Blush	☐	☐	☐
● Eyeliner	☐	☐	☐
● Eye shadow	☐	☐	☐
● Mascara	☐	☐	☐

Personal Grooming

	1	6	12+
● Deodorant	☐	☐	☐
● Perfume	☐	☐	☐
● Hair spray	☐	☐	☐
● Hair color (Ladies, stock up on the Loreal now!)	☐	☐	☐
● Permanent wave solution (curlers and papers)	☐	☐	☐
● Hair relaxer	☐	☐	☐

CHECK LIST ITEMS	NUMBER OF MONTHS		
	1	6	12+

Medicine Cabinet

Non Prescription Medications

	1	6	12+
● Activated charcoal (use if indicated for certain poisons)	❑	❑	❑
● Advil (Ibuprofen)	❑	❑	❑
● Aleve	❑	❑	❑
● Antacid (for stomach upset)	❑	❑	❑
● Anti-diarrhea medication (Kaopectate; Pepto-Bismol)	❑	❑	❑
● Aspirin	❑	❑	❑
● Benadryl	❑	❑	❑

Cold, Flu and Cough Remedies

	1	6	12+
● Cough drops	❑	❑	❑
● Nyquil/Dayquil	❑	❑	❑
● Hay fever/sinus	❑	❑	❑
● Hydrocortisone creme (Cortaid)	❑	❑	❑
● Laxatives for constipation	❑	❑	❑
● Motrin	❑	❑	❑
● Neosporin	❑	❑	❑
● Syrup of Ipecac (use to induce vomiting)	❑	❑	❑
● Tylenol (Acetaminophen)	❑	❑	❑
● Yeast infection medicine	❑	❑	❑

Medical Concerns for Young Children

	1	6	12+
● Band-Aids in lots of sizes	❑	❑	❑
● Children's Tylenol	❑	❑	❑
● Diaper rash cream	❑	❑	❑
● Digital thermometer for young babies	❑	❑	❑
● Ear viewer and instructions	❑	❑	❑
● Immunizations	❑	❑	❑
● Pedialyte (electrolyte fluid)	❑	❑	❑
● Specific medicines for your child (check on the shelf life of medications)	❑	❑	❑

CHECK LIST ITEMS	NUMBER OF MONTHS		
	1	6	12+

Alternative and Natural Health
(Note: Although herbal remedies are non-prescription, they can still be dangerous if used improperly. Please read all labels for directions and keep out of the reach of children.)

	1	6	12+
● Echinacea with goldenseal for colds	❑	❑	❑
● Cool cayenne for upper respiratory	❑	❑	❑
● L-Lysine for canker sores	❑	❑	❑
● Aloe for burns	❑	❑	❑
● Melatonin for insomnia	❑	❑	❑
● Zinc lozenges for sore throats	❑	❑	❑

Medical Supplies

	1	6	12+
● Ammonia	❑	❑	❑
● Glucose	❑	❑	❑
● Hydrogen peroxide	❑	❑	❑
● Insect bite/sting topical medicine	❑	❑	❑
● Insect repellent	❑	❑	❑
● Iodine	❑	❑	❑
● Petroleum jelly	❑	❑	❑
● Rubbing alcohol	❑	❑	❑

Hormones

	1	6	12+
● Hormone replacement medications	❑	❑	❑
● Yeast infection medication	❑	❑	❑
● Wild yam cream	❑	❑	❑

First Aid Kit

	1	6	12+
● 2-inch sterile gauze pads (4-6)	❑	❑	❑
● 2-inch sterile roller bandages (3 rolls)	❑	❑	❑
● 3-inch sterile roller bandages (3 rolls)	❑	❑	❑
● 4-inch sterile gauze pads (4-6)	❑	❑	❑
● Aloe	❑	❑	❑
● Antiseptic	❑	❑	❑
● Assorted sizes of safety pins	❑	❑	❑

CHECK LIST ITEMS	NUMBER OF MONTHS		
	1	6	12+
● Cleansing agent/soap	☐	☐	☐
● Elastic wrap	☐	☐	☐
● Eye wash	☐	☐	☐
● Hypo allergenic adhesive tape	☐	☐	☐
● Instant ice/Heat pack	☐	☐	☐
● Iodine swabs	☐	☐	☐
● Latex gloves (2 pair)	☐	☐	☐
● Moistened towelettes	☐	☐	☐
● Needle	☐	☐	☐
● Scissors	☐	☐	☐
● Splint	☐	☐	☐
● Sterile adhesive bandages in assorted sizes	☐	☐	☐
● Sunscreen	☐	☐	☐
● Thermometer	☐	☐	☐
● Tongue blades (2)	☐	☐	☐
● Trauma scissors	☐	☐	☐
● Triangular bandages (3)	☐	☐	☐
● Tube of petroleum jelly or other lubricant	☐	☐	☐
● Tweezers	☐	☐	☐

Garage

	1	6	12+
● Dog/cat food in airtight containers (like metal garbage cans) to keep rodents out	☐	☐	☐
● Kitty litter	☐	☐	☐
● Pet supplies (vitamins, pet medications like heartworm preventative, flea and tick treatments, chew toys, shampoo, etc.)	☐	☐	☐
● Back up generator	☐	☐	☐
● Fuel (gasoline, propane, etc.)	☐	☐	☐
● CB radio	☐	☐	☐
● Short wave radio	☐	☐	☐
● Work gloves	☐	☐	☐

Bug extermination

	1	6	12+
● Ant, roach, spider killer	☐	☐	☐
● Bee/wasp killer	☐	☐	☐

CHECK LIST ITEMS	NUMBER OF MONTHS		
	1	6	12+
● Rat/mouse traps	❑	❑	❑
● Fly traps	❑	❑	❑

Office

Complete family medical records *(fill in family members' names and check when completed)*

	1	6	12+
Name: _____	❑	❑	❑
Name: _____	❑	❑	❑
Name: _____	❑	❑	❑
Name: _____	❑	❑	❑
Name: _____	❑	❑	❑
Name: _____	❑	❑	❑
Name: _____	❑	❑	❑
Name: _____	❑	❑	❑
Name: _____	❑	❑	❑
Name: _____	❑	❑	❑

Documents

	1	6	12+
● Birth certificate	❑	❑	❑
● Social Security card and history	❑	❑	❑
● Marriage license	❑	❑	❑
● Divorce papers	❑	❑	❑
● Church/religious records (Baptism, Confirmation, First Communion)	❑	❑	❑
● Tax records	❑	❑	❑
● Deeds, titles, proofs of ownership	❑	❑	❑
● Insurance policies	❑	❑	❑
● Homeowners	❑	❑	❑
● Auto	❑	❑	❑
● Life	❑	❑	❑
● Health	❑	❑	❑

CHECK LIST ITEMS	NUMBER OF MONTHS		
	1	6	12+
Financial			
• Bank statements	❑	❑	❑
• Pensions	❑	❑	❑
• Investment records	❑	❑	❑
• Mortgages	❑	❑	❑
• Credit/debit cards	❑	❑	❑
• Automatic deposits/payments	❑	❑	❑
Educational Documentation			
• Certificates	❑	❑	❑
• Diplomas	❑	❑	❑
• Licenses	❑	❑	❑
• Transcripts	❑	❑	❑

Bedroom

Birth control

	1	6	12+
• Birth control pills	❑	❑	❑
• Condoms	❑	❑	❑
• Lubricant	❑	❑	❑
• Diaphragm foam	❑	❑	❑
• Info on natural family planning	❑	❑	❑
• Home pregnancy tests	❑	❑	❑

Pregnancy

	1	6	12+
• Maternity clothes	❑	❑	❑
• Antacids (high calcium)	❑	❑	❑
• Prenatal vitamins	❑	❑	❑

Childbirth

	1	6	12+
• Midwife information/home birth	❑	❑	❑
• Clean shower curtain to protect bedding	❑	❑	❑
• Info for husbands if they have to deliver the baby	❑	❑	❑
• Emergency home birth kit (list contents)	❑	❑	❑

CHECK LIST ITEMS	NUMBER OF MONTHS		
	1	6	12+

Nursing
- Manual breast pump ☐ ☐ ☐
- Bottles and nipples (disposable liners) ☐ ☐ ☐
- Sterilizing equipment ☐ ☐ ☐
- Breast pads (washable) ☐ ☐ ☐
- Nursing bras ☐ ☐ ☐

Baby Products
- Disposable diapers in various sizes ☐ ☐ ☐
- Cloth diapers ☐ ☐ ☐
- Pins or clips ☐ ☐ ☐
- Rubber pants ☐ ☐ ☐
- Baby wipes ☐ ☐ ☐
- Baggies for disposing dirty diapers ☐ ☐ ☐

Nursery
Layette
- Receiving blankets ☐ ☐ ☐
- Bath products ☐ ☐ ☐

Kids' Rooms
- Flashlight ☐ ☐ ☐
- Books ☐ ☐ ☐
- Batteries ☐ ☐ ☐
- Writing paper, pens ☐ ☐ ☐

Guest Room
- Flashlight ☐ ☐ ☐
- Extra toothbrushes, soap, towels, etc. ☐ ☐ ☐
- Sheets ☐ ☐ ☐
- Pillows ☐ ☐ ☐

Garden
- Non hybrid seeds ☐ ☐ ☐
- Herbs ☐ ☐ ☐
- Vegetables ☐ ☐ ☐

CHECK LIST ITEMS	NUMBER OF MONTHS		
	1	6	12+

- Flowers ☐ ☐ ☐
- Fruit trees ☐ ☐ ☐
- Flower bulbs ☐ ☐ ☐
- Shovel ☐ ☐ ☐
- Spade ☐ ☐ ☐
- Hoe ☐ ☐ ☐
- Fertilizer ☐ ☐ ☐
- Insecticide (natural, when possible) ☐ ☐ ☐

Family Room/Den

- Decks of playing cards ☐ ☐ ☐
- Board games ☐ ☐ ☐
- Puzzles ☐ ☐ ☐
- Children's books ☐ ☐ ☐
- Arts and crafts ☐ ☐ ☐
- Needlework ☐ ☐ ☐
- Needlepoint (mesh, yarn and patterns) ☐ ☐ ☐
- Cross stitch (floss, material and patterns) ☐ ☐ ☐
- Knitting (needles, yarn and patterns) ☐ ☐ ☐

Musical Instruments
- Piano ☐ ☐ ☐
- Acoustic guitar ☐ ☐ ☐

Homeschool Supplies
- Text books ☐ ☐ ☐
- Workbooks ☐ ☐ ☐
- Encyclopedia ☐ ☐ ☐

Attic

- Various sizes of clothes for growing kids ☐ ☐ ☐
- Pants ☐ ☐ ☐
- Jackets ☐ ☐ ☐
- Shoes ☐ ☐ ☐
- Sleeping bags ☐ ☐ ☐

CHECK LIST ITEMS	NUMBER OF MONTHS		
	1	6	12+

Workshop
- Plastic sheeting (for leaks) | ❏ | ❏ | ❏ |
- Nylon rope | ❏ | ❏ | ❏ |
- Wrench | ❏ | ❏ | ❏ |
- Hammer | ❏ | ❏ | ❏ |
- Screwdrivers | ❏ | ❏ | ❏ |
- Pliers | ❏ | ❏ | ❏ |
- Ax or hatchet | ❏ | ❏ | ❏ |
- Shovel | ❏ | ❏ | ❏ |
- Saw | ❏ | ❏ | ❏ |
- Non electric mower | ❏ | ❏ | ❏ |
- Non electric hedge clippers | ❏ | ❏ | ❏ |

Library
"How to" books
- First Aid Manual | ❏ | ❏ | ❏ |
- Physicians Desk Reference (guide to prescription drugs) | ❏ | ❏ | ❏ |
- Medical info (i.e., Merck Manual) | ❏ | ❏ | ❏ |
- Home "Fix it" Books | ❏ | ❏ | ❏ |
- Garden | ❏ | ❏ | ❏ |
- Cookbooks | ❏ | ❏ | ❏ |
- Cooking with Food Storage | ❏ | ❏ | ❏ |
- Bible | ❏ | ❏ | ❏ |
- Biographies | ❏ | ❏ | ❏ |
- Mysteries | ❏ | ❏ | ❏ |
- Classics | ❏ | ❏ | ❏ |

Hallway
- Lights | ❏ | ❏ | ❏ |
- Light bulbs | ❏ | ❏ | ❏ |
- Smoke alarm | ❏ | ❏ | ❏ |
- Carbon monoxide detector (if using alternative heat) | ❏ | ❏ | ❏ |
- Battery operated clock | ❏ | ❏ | ❏ |

CHECK LIST ITEMS	NUMBER OF MONTHS		
	1	6	12+

Patio/Deck
● Grill (charcoal, gas) ❑ ❑ ❑

Storage Shed
● Safe ❑ ❑ ❑
● Barter items ❑ ❑ ❑

(Feel free to add any other items that you want to remember for your family!)

.... ❑ ❑ ❑
.... ❑ ❑ ❑
.... ❑ ❑ ❑
.... ❑ ❑ ❑
.... ❑ ❑ ❑
.... ❑ ❑ ❑
.... ❑ ❑ ❑
.... ❑ ❑ ❑
.... ❑ ❑ ❑
.... ❑ ❑ ❑
.... ❑ ❑ ❑
.... ❑ ❑ ❑
.... ❑ ❑ ❑
.... ❑ ❑ ❑
.... ❑ ❑ ❑
.... ❑ ❑ ❑
.... ❑ ❑ ❑
.... ❑ ❑ ❑
.... ❑ ❑ ❑
.... ❑ ❑ ❑
.... ❑ ❑ ❑
.... ❑ ❑ ❑
.... ❑ ❑ ❑

Recommended Top 5 Y2K Books

Time Bomb 2000: *What the Year 2000 Computer Crisis means to You!*. Ed Yourdon and Jennifer Yourdon, Prentice Hall Computer Books; ISBN: 0130952842

The Millennium Bug: *How to Survive the Coming Chaos* Michael Hyatt, Regnery Pub; ISBN: 0895263734

Y2K: The Millennium Bug
Shaunti Feldhahn, Multnomah Publishers Inc.; ISBN: 1576734706

Spiritual Survival During the Y2K Crisis
Steve Farrar, Thomas Nelson; ISBN: 0785273093

Men Are from Mars, Women Are from Venus: *A Practical Guide for Improving Communication and Getting What You Want in Your Relationships.* John Gray, HarperCollins; ISBN: 006016848X

Preparedness Books: Top Ten List

Making the Best of Basics: Family Preparedness Handbook
by James Talmage Stevens, Gold Leaf Press; ISBN: 1882723252, 1-800-838-8854, (discount)

Encyclopedia of Country Living: An Old Fashioned Recipe Book
by Carla Emery, Sasquatch Books; ISBN: 0912365951. Much, much more than a recipe book.

Whatcha Gonna Do If the Grid Goes Down? Preparing Your Household For the Year 2000
by Susan Robinson, Virtual Sage Publishing; ISBN: 0966762509, 1-877-Y2K-SAGE, PO Box 100008, Denver, CO 80250-0008.

The New Cookin' with Home Storage
by Vicki Tate, 1-435-835-8283, $14.95 plus $3 s&h, 302 East 200 North, Manti, UT 84642.
A fascinating cookbook, written for those people who look at all the cans of food in their basement and say, "What do I do with all this stuff!!"

Food Storage 101: Where Do I Begin? $11.95

Cookin' with Powdered Milk $8.50

Cookin' with Dried Eggs $6.50

Cookin' with Beans and Rice $11.95
by Peggy Layton, 1-888-835-0311, PO Box 44, Manti, UT 84642

Where There is No Doctor: A Village Health Care Handbook
by David Werner, Carol Thuman, Jane Maxwell, The Hesperian Foundation; ISBN: 0942364155, PO Box 1692, Palo Alto, CA 94302. The basics—including how to give an injection, how to treat some dislocations and fractures, the use of common drugs, and assisting at a normal delivery.

Where There is No Dentist
by Murray Dickson, The Hesperian Foundation; ISBN: 0942364058. This book is similar to the "No Doctor" book above, covering hygiene, tooth repair, extraction, etc.

Square Foot Gardening: A New Way to Garden in Less Space With Less Work
by Mel Bartholomew, Rodale Press; ISBN: 0878573410

Physician's Desk Reference
Medical Economics Data; ISBN: 1563632896. This is a compendium of package inserts from various drugs you can often find secondhand.

A Merck Manual **and/or a copy of** *Current Therapy*
Merck & Co; ISBN: 0911910875 / W. B. Saunders Co; ISBN: 072167223X. You can also find these secondhand.

Preparedness Resources: Top Five List

I have spent a lot of time researching the best products available for preparedness. One of the things I look for in a company is whether it is versatile and should be used anyway. This list of companies gets my "good housekeeping seal of approval." Is this a guarantee? Unfortunately, no. But these are the things I am using for my own family. Since I know cost is a factor for many people, I also have many do-it-yourself tips and instructions on my Website at www.y2kwomen.com.

Many of these companies are supportive of Y2K Women, so please mention our name. Some of them will give a discount or free gift to Y2KWomen so if they ask for a code just use y2kw. Thanks!

1. WATER FILTER

British Berkefeld Water Filter—removes parasites and pathogens, as well as undesirable odors and flavors: $259.00. Each filter includes four silver-impregnated ceramic filter elements. Additional replacement elements are available for just $35.00 each.

Noah's Pantry, 902 W. First Street, Claremore, OK 74017
Toll-free: 1-888-Y2K-NOAH (1-888-925-6624), (918) 343-9500, Fax (918) 342-4675, Email: mail@noahspantry.com
Safe drinking water is often taken for granted, and seldom is provision made for a safe backup supply. During emergency situations, a piped water supply may not be available, and surface water from rivers, streams, or ponds may present the only sources of water. In this case, the water may appear unclear and have an unpleasant taste, but more importantly is often a source of disease. Even clear and apparently fresh water may be polluted with disease-causing pathogens.

Noah's Pantry is the national retail sales coordinator for British Berkefeld gravity-operated survival/camping water filters. This filter system is especially designed to micro-filter a supply of safe drinking water from cisterns, ponds, streams, and other sources of questionable water. These very reliable filters are manufactured of high grade, polished stainless steel for maximum corrosion resistance, and are hygienic, durable, and easy to clean.

British Berkefeld water filters are also compact, portable, and simple to operate. Requiring no external plumbing, each filter takes only minutes to assemble and can provide up to 21 gallons of safe drinking water each day. The high-tech silver-impregnated ceramic elements feature a nominal filtration efficiency of 0.2 microns and an absolute rating of 0.5 microns which effectively blocks waterborne pathogens and clarifies the water.

These filters are in common everyday use in households across the country, and are particularly effective on private well systems. The filter elements remove rust and cloudiness, and the activated carbon core removes undesirable tastes and odors.

The ease of operation combined with a proven effectiveness at eliminating water-borne diseases such as cholera and typhoid has led to the filter being specified for field operations by many of the world's major aid and emergency relief organizations.

- Produces safe drinking water from lakes, cisterns, streams, etc.
- Designed for everyday household use, not just an occasional camping trip
- Reliable design uses gravity—no pumps to wear out
- Long lasting filter elements will produce thousands of gallons each (depending on turbidity level of the water being filtered)
- Stainless steel construction—sanitary, easy to clean, and will last longer than plastic containers. Independently tested by Spectrum Labs, University of Arizona, Clare Microbiological, Loughborough University, and Hyder. A rigorous program of independent testing of the British Berkefeld water filters ensures complete verification of all product performance claims.

2. FOOD FOR YOUR COMMUNITY

Future Foods, Inc. Making a Difference for Future Generations Around the World, 5401 Boone Avenue North, Minneapolis, MN 55428, 1-612-504-2930.

Many of you have written asking for information on how your church and community groups can get food to distribute if there is a crisis. I'm very excited about an organization I've found that I think is, literally, doing a world of good.

It's a new company called Future Foods out of Minnesota (not to be confused with a company with a similar name in Utah). Future Foods is an offshoot of a group called, Feed My Starving Children.

First, let me tell you about FMSC. FMSC is a not-for-profit organization, dedicated to providing nourishing food to starving children worldwide, while providing significant volunteer service-learning opportunities for local youth. The organization's mission is to "provide starving children with the nutrition they need to become healthy both physically and mentally." Basically, youth volunteer workers from the community package food which is then shipped to feeding agencies, orphanages, relief agencies, and the like in places such as Honduras, Venezuela, Uganda, North Korea and Sudan. This is not a program set up to entertain youth but to enable them to serve others in desperate need.

Since its inception in 1987 by Richard Proudfit, a business executive with a heart for the poor, FMSC has provided volunteer opportunities to local youth who have processed and packaged in excess of 5,500,000 highly nutritious meals.

Now, to meet the needs of Y2K, they have formed a new company called Future Foods, Inc. And the best part is, when you order from Future Foods, a portion of the proceeds of each sale goes to support FMSC to feed starving children. So in my opinion there is a double bonus of meeting needs right now and meeting needs in the not too distant future!

As with FMSC, Future Foods packages are unique, highly nutritional meals with a long storage life. They require very simple preparation—just add water (you can also add spices). The packages are fortified rice-soy casseroles that come in chicken or beef flavor. Although it is not gourmet food by any stretch of the imagination, it is still good, plain nutritional food. (I made a casserole up for my teenage girls and they thought it was okay!) A friend of mine just ordered two pallets for his church and I know that another church has ordered 10 pallets. Future Foods is gearing up production to meet the requests for food and the management of this group is tops so I have a high amount of confidence in them. Currently, there is only a 4-8 week wait for delivery. But I expect this will change quickly. If your church or community group is thinking about food for those in need, I'd suggest you call and order right away. And please mention Y2KWomen when you call—as women this is a great way to support the needs of families everywhere.

3. HOSPITAL IN A BOX

Family Physicians Home Emergency Company,
PO Box 211205, Bedford, TX 76095,
Toll free 1-877-FAM-PHYS (1-877-326-7497) or 877-485-9115.

Twelve hundred medical supplies carefully selected by a board certified family physician to cover a variety of situations. This comes with a Y2K medical prep manual and videos on how to use your supplies for common medical problems. (This is expensive— $795—but I've arranged for Y2KWomen to get it for only $495.) Since you probably won't be using all the things in the box at once, you might want to go in on it with some other families in your neighborhood or this would be good for churches and civic organizations.

4. THE KEEPER

Store Keeper, 3332 Harwood Blvd., Suite 102-D, Bedford, TX 76021, 1-888-882-1818, Ext. 30.

The Keeper can relieve the need to stock up on tampons or pads! And with The Keeper, you can go about your daily activities in virtual freedom from your period! It's great for hiking, camping, and playing sports! For those concerned about the year 2000 and its possible ramifications, The Keeper could be the solution to feminine protection needs. Since The Keeper is reusable and should last for a good 10 years or more, it's one of the most practical products available to solve this particular need.

With The Keeper, bulky pads and tampons are no longer necessary. The female scientists of Biosphere 2 chose it as their form of feminine protection while in their enclosed environment in Oracle, Arizona, in 1992.

Here's how it works: It is a natural gum rubber cup that is worn internally, holding (instead of absorbing) monthly flow. It can be worn up to 12 hours, and even overnight. To insert The Keeper, you first fold it lengthwise between your fingers. It forms a seal which keeps fluid inside the cup. It will not absorb or disrupt your natural vaginal moisture. And it will not expose you to chemicals like bleach (unlike conventional tampons, which may have bleaches and chemical residues). So, it's environmentally friendly to the earth—AND to yourself! The Keeper can hold up to one ounce of menstrual flow. (An average woman's entire monthly flow is about 2 to 4 ounces.) And it's so comfortable—you need to make sure not to forget you're wearing it! To remove it you simply pinch the bottom of the cup to release the seal, then bear down slightly with your abdominal muscles to help move it downward. Remove slowly, and empty the contents into the toilet. Rinse or wipe, and reinsert. Between cycles, you should rinse The Keeper with sufficiently warm water and soap or a mild vinegar solution. (There is no need to boil or soak it.)

Many women find that The Keeper is very effective protection against that annoying problem—leakage. They use it alone—as their sole form of feminine protection. Once you try it, you'll learn how often you need to empty it. If you are in a situation where that isn't going to be possible for awhile, you may find that you can get by with just an added panty liner on your heaviest days, to compensate for slight leakage. It is also recommended that you use some extra protection (such as a panty liner or mini pad) when you are first trying out The Keeper just to make sure. Once you get used to using it, you'll know exactly what you require, of course. If you have ever had a vaginal child birth, order style "A" (for "After" vaginal child birth). If you have had cesarean births only, or no child births, order style "B" (for "Before" vaginal child birth). Before vaginal child birth, the vaginal walls are firmer than after. Therefore, style "A" is slightly larger in diameter and the rubber is slightly softer than that of style "B."

Besides its comfort and high-level protection, The Keeper brings economy. You could be spending $50 or more every year on disposable pads and tampons. The Keeper costs $35 + $2 s&h. And it has a life expectancy of at least 10 years. That makes it an excellent investment in your health and physical comfort! But you may try it RISK FREE. If you are not completely satisfied with The Keeper, you may return it within 3 months for a full refund, less shipping and handling.

5. COOKING

Solar oven

Global Sun Ovens (800) 408-7919, 39W835 Midan Drive, Elburn, IL 60119, Fax 630 208-7386.

When a Global Sun Oven is focused in the sun, the interior of the oven is heated by the sun's energy. Sunlight, both direct and from the reflectors, enters the oven chamber through the glass door and turns to heat energy when it is absorbed by the black inner-shell and levelator. This heat input causes the temperature inside the oven to rise until the heat loss of the oven is equal to the solar heat gain. The light energy that is absorbed by dark pots and the oven's dark interior is converted into longer wavelength heat energy and radiates from the interior materials. Most of this radiant energy is of a longer wavelength and cannot pass back out through the glass

What is the cooking temperature range?

The Global Sun Oven will reach temperatures of 360° to 400° Fahrenheit. The oven will generally reach its maximum temperature as it is being preheated. The temperature will drop when food is placed in the chamber.

How long does it take?

Cooking times are close to the same as those in a conventional oven. Because the sun is often trying to run away and hide behind clouds, cooking times can vary. At times it may take a little longer. The factors that affect the cooking time are the quality of the sunlight at the time you are cooking, the types and quantities of the food being cooked, and how often the oven is being refocused.

Does a Global Sun Oven require special pots and pans?

No, but dark thin-walled pots with lids work best. Price: $229 and it comes with a free roasting pan when you mention Y2K Women.

Volcano Cook Stove and Manuals

Call 1-800-528-0559. To get this, please use confirmation number: V-KA-02.

Year 2000 Project, WAVE Publications, P.O. Box 84902, Phoenix, AZ 85071.

Here's what my friend wrote about the volcano stove:

What is a Volcano cook stove? Briefly, it's a highly efficient charcoal or wood fueled B-B-Q type cooker that allows you to boil, grill, fry, or bake using a fraction of the fuel that other systems use. You can cook an entire meal with as little as 6 briquettes (even a Thanksgiving turkey dinner can be cooked with 12!)—less than one tenth the fuel that you would use on a conventional charcoal grill and far less than what you would use in a wood cook stove. Plus, it's so efficient that the outside of the Volcano only gets warm to the touch and can be used safely on top of a plastic table cloth! (Note: *the Volcano Emergency Cook Stove should be used outside and should not be used to heat your home.*)

For Y2K preparation, natural gas may or may not be available and so it should not be relied upon. Propane is a good short-term solution if you can put in a propane tank (500 gallons plus) at your location (beware of propane cook stoves that don't allow you to use the oven without electricity!). Understand, if major infrastructure is not restored within a few months you will use up all of your propane. Wood stoves are reliable for the long-term, but wood stoves aren't ideal, either. Modern wood heating stoves only get hot enough to simmer water—even the best wood cook stoves, costing $5,000 to $7,000 including a chimney system, are not suited for every cooking situation. There is just no way I would want a wood stove's heat blasting through the house in the middle of summer (in the past, outdoor kitchens with a second wood cook stove were common—a good, but expensive solution). And, unless you are planning to cook all day, cooking on a wood stove uses a lot of wood . . . fuel you may well want to conserve for an emergency.

Why is the Volcano Emergency Cook Stove Package so good compared to other cooking options during a crisis? Because all the parts are designed from the ground up to work together as a system so it's safe, economical, and easy to use. My wife thinks it's great. In normal times it serves as an excellent barbecue for picnics. You can fit the optional extra-tall Dutch oven (an option I highly recommend!) right into the stove to allow you to cook three whole chickens or even a Thanksgiving turkey! And with the Volcano Emergency Cook Stove Package you can cook the potatoes, vegetables, gravy or whatever else is on the menu while the turkey is roasting!

How fast does the Volcano Emergency Cook Stove Package cook? Light the briquettes on a paper towel and you can be ready to cook in as little as 10 minutes. Pop in your chicken and in less than an hour, your dinner is ready. Temperatures in a Dutch oven are easily regulated by the air-intake damper (12 briquettes gives you 2 hours of cooking time—a four pound chicken cooks in 50 minutes!). Remember, with the tall Dutch oven accessory, you can cook all the side dishes right along with your main dish—that's real time and fuel economy!

Along with the Volcano Emergency Cook Stove Package I recommend storing charcoal briquettes. (You can use small chunks of wood in the Volcano if you want, but briquettes are easier to use and, because the Volcano is so efficient, a full year's supply is remarkably inexpensive and the briquettes take up very little space. Furthermore, briquettes are safe to store—far safer than explosive propane or white gas used in other portable stoves!)

What are some other options for cooking when the power and other utilities aren't working? A fairly good short-term alternative is a propane gas grill with a stove burner on the side. These cost $150 to $350 (use only the burner in an emergency because the grill uses too much fuel for the amount of cooking!). If you go with this option, make certain to store plenty of propane bottles (10 filled tanks cost $300) and don't store them inside because of the explosion risk. Altogether, this is a $500 short-term solution. Sooner or later you are going to run out of propane (and you certainly don't have the cooking versatility that the Volcano Emergency Cook Stove Package offers).

That's why my wife and I were very excited (maybe I should say relieved—cooking without electricity or natural gas is a major problem in a crisis!) to find the Volcano Emergency Cook Stove Package. It's as easy to use as a barbecue (with far greater cooking versatility!), portable (the whole package plus the recommended extra tall Dutch oven weighs around 40 pounds and it comes in its own nylon carrying case!), economical to use (which means we are able to store literally years of charcoal briquettes for a fraction of the expense of the other cooking options), and it's also very reasonably priced. I also asked that the manufacturer include a FREE Dutch oven cookbook with each order that shows you how easy the Dutch oven is to use with the Volcano Emergency Cook Stove Package. The cookbook is called Log Cabin Dutch Oven and it tells you how to make everything from chili to Thanksgiving dinner, from breakfast to mouth-watering desserts, and from quick biscuits to fresh whole-wheat bread in your Dutch oven.

Because I want to encourage you to make what may well be a life-saving purchase (being able to cook in a crisis is absolutely essential), **I am also including two FREE reports along with the Volcano Emergency Cook Stove Package.**

Report #1: a FREE copy of what I consider to be the most important and crucial information about food storage as we face the Year 2000 Computer Crisis—the *Eating After the Crash* manual (a $79 value). This manual tells how to go to local sources to assemble a food storage program for individual families. It also details how to buy, store and use the most cost-effective foods in your area in the event of an extensive emergency. In short, it is THE information that complements the Volcano Emergency Cook Stove Package.

Report #2: a FREE special report called *Fuel-Saving Fireless*

Cooking: How Anyone Can Easily Make a Super-Efficient Fireless Slow Cooker. This little known technique of fireless cooking allows you to heat your food up once (use your Volcano stove) and then place it in the specially constructed highly insulated fireless cooker (full, easy-to-understand details for the construction of this amazing device are given in the report!). The fireless cooker keeps the food at cooking temperatures for hours—thus dramatically reducing your cooking fuel consumption and reducing wasted heat (or worse, unwanted heat in your house during the summer months!). Using this simple device can reduce your cooking fuel storage requirements by three fourths or more! And all the necessary details for the fireless cooker's low-cost construction (about $10 or less) are included in this concise report.

The only way for me to get you the special package price on the Volcano Emergency Cook Stove Package, the specially made tall Dutch oven (for cooking up to three whole chickens, a turkey, or an entire full course meal using the special rack included with the oven), and the FREE how-to cookbook is to take the orders myself.

The Volcano Emergency Cook Stove Package and the special reports ordinarily sell for over $355. But because we are coming to the manufacturer as a group (that's why the orders have to go through my company, WAVE Publications) you are able to purchase the Volcano package including the manual for only $249 plus $22.50 shipping and handling—a $106 savings. I also strongly encourage you to purchase the $94.95 (plus $12.50 shipping and handling) extra tall Dutch oven that's specifically designed for use with the Volcano stove and allows you to cook multiple course meals at the same time. It's well worth the extra money.

Internet Sites for Information
and Y2K Up-to-Date Articles

To the best of my knowledge, this information is current as of January 1999.

1. **American Red Cross,**
   http://www.redcross.org/disaster/safety/y2k.html
   Emergency preparedness information.

2. **Christian Broadcasting Network,**
   http://www.cbn.org/y2k
   Y2K resource center gives you broad overview and insights into Y2K.

3. **Communications,** http://www.rv-y2k.org/rvcecom.htm
   Alternative communications in the event of a failure of the telephone system.

4. **Daily News Coverage,** http://www.y2knews.com
   Comprehensive, global info on Y2K in print as well as on the Internet.

5. **Economic Concerns About Y2K,** http://www.yardeni.com
   Comprehensive from respected Wall Street economist Edward Yardeni.

6. **Ed Yourdon, Time Bomb 2000,** http://www.yourdon.com
   Informative and practical site.

7. **Educational Resource,** http://www.y2knet.com
   Online briefing site.

8. **Electric Utility Industry,** http://www.euy2k.com
   Dedicated to the impact of Y2K by Rick Cowles.

9. **Gary North,** http://www.garynorth.com
   Exhaustive documentation of Y2K problem.

10. **General Preparedness Information**,
    http://www.y2kchaos.com

11. **General Preparedness**,
    http://www.forums.cosmoaccess.net/forum/survival/prep/
    survival.htm
    Easy information.

12. **General Preparedness**, http://www.y2kwatch.com
    Balanced information to help individuals prepare "spiritually,
    physically and financially."

13. **General Y2K Information**, http://www.y2ktoday.com
    The world's largest Y2K site to sound a public wake-up call.

14. **Health and Medicine**, http://www.rx2000.org
    Y2K issues relating to the health and medical industry.

15. **Jim Lord**, http://www.survivey2k.com
    General survival and technical information.

16. **Joseph Project 2000**, http://www.josephproject2000.org
    Dedicated to preparing the Church to serve during Y2K by
    working with local Christians. Shaunti Feldhahn.

17. **Medical Questions**, http://www.survival-center.com/
    med-faq/intro.htm?=No+Frames
    Survival Medical FAQ (Frequently Asked Questions).

18. **Michael Hyatt, The Millennium Bug**,
    http://www.michaelhyatt.com
    Y2K awareness and information.

19. **Preparedness Information**, http://www.readyfory2k.com
    Ed Yourdon and James Stevens, *Making the Best of Basics*
    preparedness information.

20. **Rep. Stephen Horn,**
    http://www.house.gov/reform/gmit/y2k/
    Rep. Stephen Horn, Chairman of the House Subcommittee
    on Government Management, Information, and Technology
    issues Federal Government Report Cards on Y2K progress.

21. **Senator Bob Bennett,** http://www.senate.gov/~bennett
    Senator Bob Bennett—Utah.

22. **The Cassandra Project,**
    http://www.cassandraproject.org/home.html
    Committed to helping individuals and communities prepare.

23. **US Senate Committee,**
    http://www.senate.gov/~y2k/index.html
    The United States Senate Special Committee on the Year
    2000 Technology Problem.

24. **Westergaard Site,** http://www.y2k timebomb.com
    John Westergaard's dealing with infrastructure concerns like
    utilities, telecommunications, banking, etc.

25. **Y2K Helpful Background Article,** *Vanity Fair* Article
    http://www.remarq.com/default/transcript.pl?group=comp.
    software.year-2000:50034064:50034064&update=1770.

:::

Suppliers

(Please mention Y2KWomen.)

Baygen Radio, http://www.ccrane.com/index.html

Y2K Prep Foods, http://www.y2kprep.com/food.htm

Food Storage, Millennium III Foods,
http://www.millennium3foods.com/
1-888-883-1603, Commercial Food Storage Site.

Water and Food Storage, Noah's Pantry,
http://www.noahspantry.com
Commercial water filter.

Lighting and Oil Lamps, http://www.oillampman.com

Renewable Energy, http://www.jademountain.com or
http://www.realgoods.com

Solar Batteries,
http://www.mtmarketplace.com/solarcharger.html

Solar Box Cookers,
http://www.accessone.com/~sbcn/spasteur.htm

Solar Energy, http://www.solardome.com/SolarDome80.html

Solar Information, http://www.windsun.com/info_index.htm

Y2K Power Back Up & Alternatives,
http://www.y2knapa.com/altenergy.html
::

Government Resources

CIO Council Year 2000 Information Directory
http://www.itpolicy.gsa.gov/mks/yr2000/y2khome.htm
General Services Administration/CIO Council Year 2000
Information directory provides up-to-date information as well as
links to federal agency and state Y2K Websites.

Dept. of Housing and Urban Development Y2K Website
http://www.hud.gov/cio/year2000/

Environmental Protection Agency Year 2000 Website
http://www.epa.gov/year2000/index.htm

FDIC Year 2000 Project
http://www.fdic.gov/about/y2k/
Information on financial institutions and the work being done to
bring their computer systems into compliance for the Year 2000.

Federal Aviation Administration's Year 2000 Website
http://www.faay2k.com/

Federal Communications Commission Year 2000 Page
http://www.fcc.gov/year2000/
The purpose of this Website is to provide an information
resource for communications and broadcasting companies
(and their customers) who are concerned about the Year 2000
problem. This site provides specific information on both FCC
activities and industry activities, including those of industry
associations.

Federal Highway Administration Year 2000 Website
http://www.fhwa.dot.gov/y2k/index.htm

Federal Emergency Management Agency
http://www.fema.gov/y2k/
Y2K emergency information

FEMA on Y2K for kids
http://www.fema.gov/kids/y2k.htm

GAO Reports
http://www.gao.gov/y2kr.htm
Year 2000 Computing Crisis and other GAO Publications

**General Services Administration Y2K Telecommunications
Website**
http://y2k.fts.gsa.gov/
The latest Y2K compliance information about telecommunications products and services for federal, state, local and tribal government telecommunications managers.

Health Care Financing Administration Y2K Website
http://www.hcfa.gov/y2k/
Information on Medicare and Medicaid systems.

National Institute of Standards and Technology Year 2000 Page
http://www.nist.gov/y2k/index.htm
The National Institute of Standards and Technology's
Information Technology Laboratory (ITL) has been working on
various aspects of the Year 2000 problem over the past two years,
particularly in the areas of testing and defining standards for
testing Year 2000 features.

Nuclear Regulatory Commission (NRC) Y2K Planning
http://www.nrc.gov/NRC/NEWS/year2000.html
The Nuclear Regulatory Commission is pursuing a comprehensive program for dealing with the Y2K problem, ensuring that
NRC's computer systems supporting the agency will function
properly, and those licensed by the NRC to use nuclear materials, including utilities operating nuclear power plants, will identi-
fy and rectify any Y2K problems with their computer systems
before January 1, 2000.

Office of Management and Budget Year 2000 Progress Report
http://www.cio.gov/598rpt.html
Overall, the Federal government continues to make progress in
addressing the year 2000 problem but the rate for some agencies
is still not fast enough. This report summarizes actions as of
May 15, 1998.

Securities Exchange Commission Year 2000 Page
http://www.sec.gov/news/home2000.htm
Information on SEC and the Year 2000 computer systems compliance with regard to both internal systems and market regulation.

Small Business Administration
http://www.sbaonline.sba.gov/y2k/
Guidance in addressing organizational Y2K vulnerabilities.

Social Security Administration Y2K Information
http://www.ssa.gov/facts/y2knotic.html

U.S. Senate Special Committee on the Year 2000 Technology Problem
http://www.senate.gov/~y2k/index.html
The purpose of the special committee is 1) to study the impact of the Year 2000 technology problem on the executive and judicial branches of the federal government, state governments, and private sector operations in the United States and abroad; 2) to make such findings of fact as are warranted and appropriate; and 3) to make such recommendations, including recommendations for new legislation and amendments to existing laws and any administrative or other actions, as the special committee may determine to be necessary or desirable.

US Department of Education Year 2000 Page
http://www.ed.gov/offices/OCIO/year/
The Year 2000 is coming soon, and the education community must be prepared. At stake is the utility and preservation of the information systems and data that all entities, public and private, that have automated their work processes rely on to function.

Y2K Task Force for Canadian Government/Industry
http://strategis.ic.gc.ca/sc_mangb/y2k/engdoc/homepage.html
Website of Canadian federal government/industry task force to deal with Year 2000 computer problem.

Year 2000 Assessment Guide
http://www.gao.gov/special.pubs/y2kguide.pdf
General Accounting Office's Year 2000 Computing Crisis: An Assessment Guide serves as a guide for developing a Y2K compliance project checklist. NOTE: This links DIRECTLY to a PDF document that requires the free Adobe Acrobat Reader software to read it.

Year 2000 Canadian Federal Government Site
http://www.info2000.gc.ca/
Information on Canadian federal government's work to prepare itself and the country for the Year 2000 computer problem.

About Karen Anderson and Y2KWomen

Karen Anderson, M.S., is the founder of Y2KWomen, an organization to promote Y2K awareness and information on the special needs and concerns of women.

After getting over her own personal skepticism and disbelief, Karen began to see the need for women to prepare for a potential crisis situation. She is now working full time to help women to become aware of the Y2K problem, how to prepare for the consequences of Y2K, and how to cope with it emotionally.

Karen's background makes her uniquely qualified to discuss issues around Y2K because of her background as a Marriage and Family Therapist. She received her B.A. from Taylor University in Psychology and Social Work and her M.S. in Family and Community Development from the University of Maryland. She did her graduate clinical training in Marriage and Family Therapy.

Karen has recently written a Special Report entitled, *The Year 2000 Computer Problem: The 10 Things Every Woman Must Do Now to Keep Her Family Safe* and an audio tape album: *The Busy Woman's Guide to Preparing for Y2K*.

Karen and her husband, Steve, have been married for 23 years, have two teenage daughters, and live in Texas. They also have a Wheaten Scottie dog named McDuff (who's cute but not the brightest dog in the world!). They are members of Colleyville Presbyterian Church (PCA).

For more information, see www.y2kwomen.com or to order please call 1 877-Y2K-4WOMEN (1 877-925-4966).

For even more information order Karen's:
"The Busy Woman's Guide to Preparing for Y2K"

This album of six audio tapes (approximately 50 minutes each) is designed to give you the best information available in the shortest amount of time. In this set you'll get the six audio cassettes plus an edited transcription of each tape so you can listen to the tape and not have to worry about taking notes or missing vital information! Here's what you'll get in the audio tape album:

The Busy Woman's Guide to: Making your Home Y2K Friendly: An interview with Cris Evatt, co-author of the book, *30 Days to a Simpler Life.* How to organize your home, learn what to keep, where to keep it, what to recycle and what to save for barter and charity.

Living Without Electricity: What a Normal Family Needs to Know: An interview with Susan Robinson, author of *Whatcha Gonna Do If the Grid Goes Down?* Find out the things an average family needs to think through in preparing for what it would be like to spend more than just a few hours without power.

Cooking with Food Storage: Now What Do I Do?: An interview with Vicki Tate, author of *The New Cookin' with Food Storage.* Learn what is different about cooking with food storage and the specific steps you need to take now to integrate it into your family's life before a crisis.

Non-Prescription Remedies—How to Make an Herbal First Aid Kit: An interview with master herbalist Robin Lockwood. Learn exactly what you need to have on hand to take care of health problems if you can't get traditional medicines.

Feminine Protection: Finally a Solution: An interview with Dena Waldrop, manager of The Keeper Store. Find out what the alternatives are and how to not worry about this very sensitive and awkward issue.

The Church's Response to Y2K: An interview with Shaunti Feldhahn, founder of "The Joseph Project 2000" and author of *Y2K: The Millennium Bug—A Balanced Christian Response.* Learn what you can do to get your church involved without having to "reinvent the wheel." Also, get answers to some of the tough questions facing women today who truly want to be light in a dark world.

Here's what just a few women have to say about Karen's groundbreaking new audio series:

"These tapes contain wisdom that, if used, will not only save you money, but save you a whole lot of time—a precious commodity as the clock ticks towards the new millennium. I highly recommend them."
Joann Tippery, WA

"Karen has done a remarkable service in bringing together some of the best experts available to help women in the real world of everyday life. The women Karen interviews are wonderful examples of the positive power of 'women helping women.' I found these tapes a great source of comfort and reassurance that every woman who is concerned about protecting her family should have."
Sharon North, AR

"With so much to do and so little time, it's great to find a resource that can help me handle the day to day challenges of work, motherhood and preparing for Y2K. The information contained in these tapes gave me hope when I was feeling overwhelmed. I couldn't be more thankful."
Janice Haner, AR

"I love my husband dearly, but there are some things that men just don't think about. Fortunately, Karen has not only thought ahead but she's come up with an answer before I've even thought of the question! Her time and effort in making these tapes has made my job so much easier. I'm very grateful for this very valuable information."
Tina Gilchrist, TX

Order *"The Busy Woman's Guide to Preparing for Y2K"* **audio tapes** now for only $79.95 (plus $4.95 shipping) and save $10 off the normal $89.95 retail price.

To place your order by major credit card, call us toll free at 1-877-Y2K-4WOMEN (1-877-925-4966) and mention your book discount or order online at www.y2kwomen.com.

Your support goes to help reach women everywhere in preparing for Y2K! By working together and helping each other we can make a difference.

THIS SPACE RESERVED FOR YOUR PERSONAL Y2K NOTES

THIS SPACE RESERVED FOR YOUR PERSONAL Y2K NOTES

THIS SPACE RESERVED FOR YOUR PERSONAL Y2K NOTES

ALSO AVAILABLE TO GET YOU PREPARED FOR Y2K

The Millennium Bug: How to Survive the Coming Chaos
By Michael S. Hyatt
In this *New York Times* best-seller, Michael S. Hyatt explains the impending Y2K catastrophe in simple terms and gives thirteen specific action steps to protect you and your family.
0-89526-334-3 • Hardcover • 228 pages
Also available on video: 0-7852-9447-3

The Senate Special Report on Y2K:
Investigating the Impact of the Year 2000 Problem
By Senator Robert F. Bennett and Senator Christopher J. Dodd
This long-awaited Y2K report from the U.S. Senate summarizes potential problems facing the most vital areas affecting our everyday lives: electricity, telecommunications, water, and more.
0-7852-6851-0 • Paperback • 228 pages

Spiritual Survival During the Y2K Crisis
By Steve Farrar
Best-selling author Steve Farrar examines Y2K through the lens of biblical truth and helps you discover a practical plan for your family.
0-7852-7309-3 • Paperback • 252 pages

The Y2K Personal Survival Guide
By Michael S. Hyatt
This one-stop, comprehensive book by best-selling author Michael S. Hyatt explains the ins-and-outs of Y2K preparation—everything you need to know to get you and your family from this side of the crisis to the other.
0-89526-301-7 • Hardcover • 360 pages

Y2K: The Day the World Shut Down
By Michael Hyatt and George Grant
A chilling novel about what could happen in the year 2000 when the world's computers shut down.
0-8499-1387-X • Paperback • 268 pages

Y2K: What Every Christian Should Know
By Michael S. Hyatt
In this special audio package, Michael S. Hyatt, author of the *New York Times* best-seller *The Millennium Bug*, talks about what the Millennium Bug is, how it will affect you, and what Christians should do personally to prepare for the coming days.
0-7852-6933-9 • Audio • Two 90-minute cassettes